ROCK SOLID
CONFIDENCE

6-25-12

Marilyn,

May you be blessed
with joy & peace. May
all the love you give
out so generously be
the source of your
inner peace & harmony!

My Best,
Jan

ROCK SOLID CONFIDENCE

PRESENTING YOURSELF WITH ASSURANCE, POISE AND POWER

JAN M. WHALEN, MASL

PERSONAL Jaz
Personal JAZ Publishing
Phoenix, Arizona

ROCK SOLID CONFIDENCE
PRESENTING YOURSELF WITH ASSURANCE, POISE AND POWER
Jan M. Whalen, MASL

Copyright © 2011 Jan M. Whalen, MASL

Published by
Personal JAZ Publishing
Phoenix, Arizona
623 466-5067
jan@personaljaz.com
http://www.personaljaz.com

This publication is designed to provide accurate and authoritative information in regard to the subject matter covered. It is sold with the understanding that the publisher is not engaged in rendering professional medical services. If professional advice or other expert assistance is required, the services of a competent professional should be sought. Some of the names and places mentioned in this book have been changed to protect the identities of the clients.

ISBN 13: 978-0-9821051-1-5
ISBN 10: 0-9821051-1-8

Cover design by Crystal McMahon
Jan's photo by Krystalyn Digioia
Page Design by Don Enevoldsen
Editing by Heather Clarke
Production Coordination by Janet Jaz

Printed in the United States of America.

THIS BOOK IS DEDICATED TO
ALICE AND L.J. WHALEN
WHO GAVE ME LIFE AND
LOVE FOR LEARNING.

CONTENTS

PREFACE

*"I am not afraid of storms for
I am learning to sail my own ship."*
— Louisa May Alcott

Who wants more confidence? No matter your age or profession, words like courage, faith, perseverance and confidence are basic necessities. My life is all about finding confidence; in fact, you could say that I'm your perfect tour guide—but not for the usual reasons.

When my kids were 12 and 14, we were all students in a Taekwondo class. Mike joined first, followed by his younger brother Scott—and three months later, I, the thirty-something mom, joined them.

For the third class, the new white belts were instructed to bring boards to break. After coming back for the second part of class, we sat along the wall of the gym. Perhaps because I was the only adult in this new group, I was *called* first. All eyes were on me as I tried and failed to break my board. I may have been the oldest in years, but my foot could not figure out how to do it, no matter how many attempts I made. I sat down with a sore ego.

All the other students, including my sons, stepped up and one by one, broke their boards and I thought, "How can these kids do it but not me?" I planned to figure it out at home, but then I heard our instructor, Master Bruce, call my name. He was going to give me one last chance to redeem myself.

Holding the board with a steel grip, he challenged me to face myself. My foot slapped the wood twice, so he stopped and

1

told me, "Don't aim for the board, aim for my chest." It seemed barbaric, but I gave it one more try. To my surprise, I could feel the jagged fibers as the board split in two. There are no words to describe the moment the impossible becomes reality.

But the true break-through happened on the way home. Scott said, "Congratulations, Mom, you broke your first board!"

"Thanks, I'm glad I finally did it, but you know, I'd give anything to have your confidence."

His next words will stay with me forever: *"Mom, don't you know? Don't you know that confidence isn't something you get from somebody else? It's something you give to yourself."*

This was the first of many Taekwondo lessons for me. As time went on, I realized what went wrong that night and caught a glimpse of the belief, the limiting factor that was present when I didn't achieve a goal. I saw others able to break their boards; in other words, I saw others reaching their goals, but I didn't *see it for myself. I lacked belief in myself. When I reached beyond the goal with passion, everything changed.* The power to break the board, to advocate for a cause, to close the deal, to speak to any group, comes from a knowing within your being—confidence.

I also realized that confidence is not given by a caring parent, a helpful teacher or a motivational speaker. It can be nurtured and applauded, but ultimately it is the free will and personal responsibility of the individual who stands up to say, "YES" to the self, to the task—to life itself.

As I said, I may be the perfect guide as my perfection is carved out of years experiencing panic attacks, puzzled looks, a few "under-whelmed" audiences, botched relationships, weak handshakes—OK, you get the point. Yes, I've had my share of successes, but I didn't know when the next brick would drop; I didn't trust myself.

Despite these pain-injected experiences and apprehension, the world of presentation calls to me every day. In fact, my own stumbling blocks have become stepping stones. So here I am, writing a book about confidence that can be applied to the confident presentation of YOU and your ideas in formal, informal and social speaking venues.

I was at a networking event recently when a chiropractor said that a good lead for his business is anyone with a spine. We laughed; we were all included. It made me realize that we each have a spine, but how many have backbone? Striving for "backbone" brings stability and character to our lives. My good friend and spiritual counselor, Rev. Cynthia Williams, unknowingly gave me a clear vision of what this book is about. Use your creative mind to visualize two types of people.

One is like an amoeba, which, if you remember from your science classes, is a shape-shifting cell that changes with its environment. When in danger, it rolls into a ball and secretes a protective coating over itself. Closed off for too long, it can die.

The second person is like a mountain. The mountain is placed upon the Earth in a certain location and no matter what happens on its surface, it remains unchanged. Its core is stable through snowstorms, forest fires, and springtime blooming. Animals and man can build homes on top of it, but nothing on the outside changes its fundamental self.

Obviously, it's better to be a mountain, yet how many situations make us feel more like an amoeba: weak, flimsy, fragile, vulnerable, inadequate, defenseless, unprotected, powerless, ineffective, uncertain, and unsettled? This is a part of our human experience, and many of us spend years protecting ourselves from a world that does not feel safe.

The goal is to be like the mountain by taking our place in the world; by being independently rock solid at our core, yet interdependently flowing, flexible and easy with our environment. The mountain is our example of self-mastery. It remains steady and welcomes any plant, tree, animal or human to it without reservation. With confidence, we can do the same.

I firmly believe that if you are reading these words, you have an important message to bring to the world and wish to develop the self-mastery it takes to accomplish your goals. Perhaps you've written your own book, have discovered something that no one else knows, been successful in some endeavor, or been promoted to a leadership position. As King George VI said in *The King's Speech*, "*...because I have a voice,*" NOW is the time to give voice to *your* accomplishments. You don't have to go through what I did. It is my honor to share what has worked for me as well as the clients I've coached over the years.

What is the mission of this book? In short, it is: *Be yourself and at the same time understand the needs of your audience; be gentle, hospitable and humane in your approach, yet add your own unique twist into each thought and word you say.*

Once you taste the joy of delivering your message, you'll view what you once tolerated or dreaded as a "gift." Join me in speaking to your inner amoeba to break down some of the common myths that stand between you and your rock solid confidence.

This is what is true for me: I am grateful for my struggles, challenges and weaknesses; they are also my area of expertise. These, as well as my triumphs, are bound in this book for your unlimited growth and happiness. Bring your best self into the mix, and together, we'll create a new and confident path for you.

4

INTRODUCTION

"Wherever I go, there I am."
— unknown

Once upon a time you were a child and life was filled with a few basic needs—all to be met by others. You could usually cry and somebody did something to help you. You couldn't walk or sit or feed yourself. Then you began to master your body and your mind: turning your head, rolling over, crawling, making words, and then making arguments as to why you need the car on Saturday night.

Self-mastery is a vital component in increasing our confidence—one that we continue to develop. Knowing that we can set goals, achieve them, and learn new things is empowering; yet mastery of the self is the glue that holds it all together.

Who among us wants confidence? Who doesn't? Confidence is a slippery animal; one moment it's with you, the next moment you wonder where it went. Almost anything you say about how to get it and how to keep it can be disputed. Is it nature, nurture or destiny?

It gets personal. You may say, "Do I deserve to be confident if I'm attempting something new?" "If she can do it better, should I even try?" "I used to do it this way; now the situation is different and nothing is working for me lately."

With questioning thoughts, we wonder and we create a space for doubt in our minds. Filled with confidence, we step out with curiosity, step out of our comfort zone and try on the new. Confidence is like a spotlight, following us everywhere we go. It is vital in all facets of our lives, especially when public speaking—which is the center of this book.

We're like big bouquets of flowers—with each flower representing a different experience. Let's look at a woman who is a teacher, mother and photographer. How many women could this describe? Probably many. However, let's look at other flowers in her bouquet: oldest of 4, married twice, board member, salesperson, editor, secretary, and so on. With each activity being represented by a different flower, we see that her life is rich with experiences and her bouquet is like no other.

For this reason, she has a right and even a duty to step out in confidence to live the fullest, most exciting life possible. There are many ways to approach this topic of confidence; however, this book will focus on the public presentation of the self and the mastery it takes to achieve that confidence.

In Part 1, we are going to walk through some of the feelings and thoughts you might have about speaking—the ones standing between you and confidence. The discussion centers on mastering yourself. Where are your particular stumbling blocks? Which old beliefs make sense on the surface, yet keep your goals slightly out of reach?

Part 2 allows you to get in touch with the real you—the person you bring to the stage, the core of your book, the sales meeting, the presentation, the friendship, the marriage. Once you can articulate your strengths, you are now ready to face the world.

In Part 3, we focus on the next part of the confidence pyramid—the audience. What do they want? The audience is your communication partner. They simultaneously receive and give you information. They give clues as to how they want to receive your message and help you decide what to say. How much attention shall you give to: order and sequence, bottom line results, building team spirit and creativity? Correct interpretation of their expectations is unlocked through listening and is a vital component of your success.

Now that we've set the stage, you're ready to play! Part 4 consists of twenty (20) commonly asked questions and their answers, with easy exercises to take your confidence from where it is to the rock solid level. Making an effort to step out of your comfort zone is the best way to nurture your confident spirit.

The concluding remarks in Part 5 round out the journey. Guidelines will be given to assist you in knowing you've reached your destination. References are given for further study as you maintain your new lifestyle of confident living.

Perhaps you'll be teaching some of the ideas shared in this book. If that happens, then my story will have the happiest of endings! Enjoy!

Rock Solid Confidence

Part 1
SELF MASTERY IS THE GOLDEN KEY

"Discipline isn't discipline when you start making exceptions."

MIKE ROELOFS, FOOTBALL AND TRACK COACH

Rock Solid Confidence

CHAPTER 1
AM I ENOUGH?

"One man (woman) with courage is a majority."
— Thomas Jefferson

I'd been looking for that trendy shoe—a cross between sandal and boot. I found a wonderful pair, but the heels were stilettos—much taller than my usual. The sales person, Tom, persuaded me to try them on anyway. So I did. Despite the fact that I felt like I was standing on my tippy toes, this new height gave me the ability to look straight into Tom's eyes. I realized I was instantly, lushly tall. He saw the gleam in my eyes and suggested that I "walk in them for awhile." So I did, and I fell in love with my new height, despite the fact that my right foot was beginning to hurt.

After much self-debate, I decided to get them. After all, *they were on sale* and (compelling reason #2), if I didn't like them, I could give them to my niece Monica, who wears the same size. Never mind she's already 5'11" and why would she want my leftover shoes? I made my decision and when I took them off I barely noticed that my left ankle was sore, and I had to take twelve steps before the kinks in each step disappeared. So I got the magic shoes and kept them until the spell was broken—thirty minutes later. My better judgment told me to take them back before I hurt myself. What was I thinking?

I'll tell you what I was thinking. I was thinking that it would be nice to have long legs to match my long feet. I was

11

thinking that I could instantly seem thinner and maybe even younger. There was a lot of thinking going on.

Mrs. Eugene McCarthy, politician's wife, once said, "I am who I am, I look the way I look and I am my age." To that, I must add, "and I am just as tall as I am, so get over it!" This is an example where the wish to be more, the fear of not being enough, and the hope of being perfect overshadowed the mastery of self acceptance.

Many of us ask these questions:

> Do I have enough beauty?
> Am I smart enough?
> Do I have the right education?

The answer is, yes and no. No, if we look out into the world for someone to validate us. If we play the ever popular comparing game, we'll always find someone who seems to have more beauty, is more credible, and does "it" better. Tim is an entrepreneur who has never been to college, yet he learned what he needed to know from other sources. He's fine as long as he doesn't compare himself to those with college degrees. With his passion, enthusiasm and success, it wouldn't even occur to most people to question where he gets his knowledge. I marvel at his resourcefulness.

We also ask questions like:

> Who will choose me?
> Will I live happily ever after?

The truth is that if you master choosing *you*— passionately, from your heart—as if all the old love songs were written by you *to you*, then sweet happiness is yours. This, of course, needs to be done without judging yourself against others, or you're right back where you started. The old saying, "We're all in this together, alone," is exactly true. If you are not honoring yourself, then no one else can know how to honor you either. You teach people how to treat you by the example you give. In order to give, you must first be able to receive. To receive you need to give yourself the feeling of worth. Fill your own cup, and you'll never have that empty, alone feeling.

THIS IS YOUR WORLD

Life is a game of self-mastery. We bring our challenges onto our own personal playing field, set up tests and call in people to make it a fun game. Some of us need to master jealousy and others fear, anger, or unconditional love. Ben Franklin said, "Pride is the hardest fault to control because, even if a person should conceive that he had properly overcome pride, he would be proud of his humility." There are many ways we judge the self and question our value. Upon mastering ourselves, we confidently invite anything we choose into our lives.

Almost every self-help book, every teacher, every financial advisor mentions the word *balance*. I agree. Before delving into any solutions, let's get real with the kind of balance we need and the thinking that keeps us from realizing our goals and dreams. What thoughts live inside us? What habits have we picked up along the way that shake our confidence and hold us in a state of insecurity?

The late John O'Donohue, poet, theologian and philosopher, tells us that there are three places in our personal universe: inside the body, outside the body, and the thresholds that connect both worlds—our five senses. Pretty simple, really. The inside is the exclusive world of self. This is the place we find our blood, bones, muscles and voice, as well as our thoughts, feelings and beliefs.

The senses allow us to touch velvet, smell pop corn, experience chocolate, hear the beauty of our own names, and see into the eyes of another. Some of us favor one sense over another and if, for instance, our hearing fails, we mysteriously compensate through a heightened awareness of another sense.

Simultaneously, the world gets to see us through the senses. It has been said that "the eyes are the windows to the soul," and the voice expresses the emotions within. On the phone, it takes two words to detect a friend's mood. We could usually tell when a fellow Taekwondo student would *not* break his board based on the *lack of* conviction we heard in the kyup (a power sound martial artists make before doing something requiring great effort). Determination on the inside is expressed on the outside.

Even though the outside world is bigger, the inside world is our universe. It is our responsibility, our temple, and the only place we have jurisdiction. It's best to learn to build self-value at an early age. Take for example a baby who brings joy to everyone who meets her.

She realizes that she makes people laugh and respond to her. Without a solid backbone—an awareness that she is not placed here solely to make others happy (or like her)—she could miss the fact that her world is within. After rehearsing this behavior for many years, she may be unaware of the fact that she has forgotten herself. She learns to be a people pleaser, or to take the moods and bad manners of others personally, waiting for outward signs of validation. Without nurturing her inner self, her confidence can never reach its rock solid core.

CHAPTER 2
LIFE HAS A PURPOSE FOR US

"Taking responsibility and solving any problem is a positive approach to correcting what we have failed to control. Taking responsibility for what we cannot control can bring unearned feelings of failure, frustration and de-motivation."
— *Connecting Peace, Purpose and Prosperity*
by Rob Severson

Because we are human, it's natural to get stuck occasionally. Challenges arise and we create our own set of excuses—many pointing to the outside world—to explain why we are not doing what we want to do or getting what we want to get. The world is filled with people who magically show up in our day to push our buttons as if they were professional trouble makers. They throw boulders upon our paths, and if it weren't for them, we would be happy, healthy, wealthy and wise. Or would we?

Let's take a look at the opposing side of conventional thought. Another way to see these "crazy makers" is to visualize them as life's representatives, who show us the gaps in our confidence and self mastery. What if they are mirrors reflecting something that is hidden within us?

This is not a new approach. Holocaust survivor, Viktor Frankl, in *Man's Search for Meaning* wrote, "What was really needed was a fundamental change in our attitude toward life. We had to learn ourselves and furthermore, we had to teach the despairing men, that *it did not really matter what we*

15

expected from life, but rather what life expected from us. We needed to stop asking about the meaning of life, and instead to think of ourselves as those who were being questioned by life—daily and hourly."

What is life expecting from us? What is our purpose in being here? If we see that "the worst of times and the best of times" come together in the same moment, we give up judging, complaining and feeling sorry for ourselves. That is when we begin to wake up to the core of our existence.

When we are not judging a difficult person or an unpleasant situation, we can see them more clearly. This allows us to realize what "life is asking of us" and by mastering ourselves, the stumbling blocks can be rearranged into our personal stepping stones, thus achieving anything we want. This is the heart of self mastery and the core of the confidence we seek.

QUESTIONS VS. QUESTIONING

Frankl mentioned that we were "questioned by life," so let's consider the subtle, yet significant differences between the words "question" and "questioning." Lack of confidence can be measured by the number of questioning questions rolling around in our heads. But, you ask, isn't it healthy to ask questions? Yes, although there is a big difference in questions that add to our confidence and those that erode our spirits. Notice the kinds of questions playing in your head. Listen again. Is the nature of the question an itemization of your past failures and weaknesses? Does it subtly place thoughts of fear and doubt about yourself in your mind? Or is it hopeful and helpful?

Note the difference between these two sets of questions:

1) Am I really ever going to reach my goals?
Am I good enough to compete?
Why is everyone better than me?
When am I going to get a break?

2) Which steps will I take to reach my goals?
What daily routine will best prepare me to compete?
How am I maximizing my skills?
Where will I go to celebrate my victories?

The first set is questioning, doubting; the second set asks a question that stimulates options for action. The first gives a feeling of helplessness; the second strength and hope.

The questioning voice inside our heads is like a seductive magician with a million ways to demonstrate our unworthiness and will recycle, invent or blow any situation out of proportion. It feeds us half truths and unfair comparisons—and lives on fear. We try to figure it all out in our heads, which never works in the end. Sadly, like gravity, it is easier to believe the questioning as it sounds logical to our minds, and this voice always makes a compelling case.

The more powerful questions are laced with positive assumptions about future success. These questions represent forward-thinking wisdom that knows that our greatest lessons come from past mistakes. A child understands vividly the word "hot" after touching the stove. We'd never wish pain upon our children or ourselves, yet when life brings lemons, let's not lose the lesson by throwing it away—instead, make the tall cool drink.

"It's human nature that the majority of people seek the meaning of life, while those who are spiritually aware embrace that it's more fulfilling to give their

life meaning. Never allow your heart to be disabled by an unworthy attitude. The thoughts you have about others are an unconscious reflection of how you feel about yourself. There is only one YOU—the value of love is the amount of life you invest in it!"

—Steven Eric Connor

CHAPTER 3

AM I WORTHY?

"In youth we learn; in age we understand."
— Marie Ebner-Schenbe

Perhaps the bottom line in pinpointing the lack of confidence is, we don't feel worthy. Another, more quiet voice inside us knows we ARE worthy, yet the un-mastered self pushes the panic button, frantically looking to others for validation. The problem is, those asked are a part of the outside world. So these fundamental questioning statements are placed in the hands of the "public"—like a popularity contest. It's like displaying a rare ruby at the mall, asking its value of anyone passing by.

In looking back at my youth, the concept of worth was mentioned quite a bit, but I never realized how it was affecting my every move. My Dad, who had a pretty tough childhood, used to tell us he felt like "a penny waiting for change" and signed his letters "Just L. J."

Before we get very far down this path, let me say that the intent here is not to blame mom and dad for every problem—poor mom and dad had their own parents to deal with. They were simply doing the best they could. My philosophy is: you can't really call yourself a grown up until you forgive your mother and father for what you *think* they did *to* you.

As the oldest child of eight, there was a lengthy discussion as to whether or not I and my brother Len, just a

19

year younger, were "college material." We entered college wondering how long we'd be able to hang on. Years later, one of the proud days for our family came at Len's graduation from Palmer College of Chiropractic, where he walked on stage to receive his doctoral degree. As we older sibs advanced from bachelors to masters degrees, questioning the quality of our "material" faded.

Some of the very brightest people in our family did not graduate from a college, yet chose other paths to use their gifts. The world is now aware that there are many kinds of intelligences, and *worthy* does not come with a college degree. Whether it's MSU, OJT or finding a master to teach you what you need to know—let your education bring you closer to your goals rather than define your worth.

As members of the human family, our net worth can never be measured in dollars or pounds or *pesos*. We have value because we are brave enough to be here upon planet Earth. When we compare ourselves to others, that's when we get into trouble. It's an apples-to-oranges thing and while the world may have jobs that require judgment, contests to win, and people who make the cut or not, there can be no comparison when we focus on the essence of who we are and the job we came here to do.

Some may argue that feeling unworthy helps us achieve more. While it's true that working for a goal is a worthy activity, without a sense of self worth and self efficacy, our belief in achieving any goal is hit and miss. When a baby can sit, then crawl, then walk, we celebrate the small steps. We see and accept "growth" in children, yet as adults, we expect that since we don't grow physically, we don't grow in other ways. In any endeavor, when we are able to make a list of the small successes along the way to our larger goals, we heal. Counting what we have gives a feeling of accomplishment, which builds hope, which gives us more enthusiasm for our goals, which speeds up the process and places us on a positive path.

Once upon a time, when I was a sixth grade teacher in Wabasha, Minnesota, there was a young girl who was very bright and earned good grades on her tests. She worried about making mistakes and would argue with me over every single error she made. When she did well, she wasn't proportionately happy about it. She seemed relieved, as if she had been saved from disaster, but rarely did I see her take joy in any A+ grade she received. My friend Betty used to say, "It's a poor frog, who can't croak around his own pond." While not poor economically, she was poor on the worthiness scale.

Sandy, another student in a different city, wore her worthlessness on the outside. She was so deeply wounded one could feel her pain. She did not participate in class. She did not talk to anyone, respond to questions, or complete her homework. She was walking misery and hung her head in class each day. Many of us, victims of our circumstances, have had such feelings.

As adults, strange behavior lurks behind feelings of unworthiness. To have the confidence to live in the world is to know we have a place here. When we don't feel worthy, we try to hide it. But, like putting a girdle on a pig, it spills out in odd sorts of ways. We sometimes brag about other people too much; we find partners with more perceived strength; we get too loud, too soft; we drink a little too much; smoke to look cool; buy too many clothes; fall short of our goals at work and wonder why. The list goes on, but you get the idea.

We might even make an unkind comment to a dear friend for no good reason. Out of the blue, and just as things are going so well, we throw the proverbial monkey wrench

21

into the mix. Self sabotage comes in many disguises, yet our subconscious belief is the same—we aren't worthy of life's abundance. Once we get an idea about ourselves, we'd rather be right than good.

Do we do this knowingly, on purpose? Do we get up in the morning saying, "How am I going to really mess things up today, because this is all I deserve?" No, I don't think it's that transparent to us. We can go years, even lifetimes unaware of any worthiness deficiencies. Lucky for us, when our lives are not working, we are forced to stop, look, listen and examine our attitude about our own self worth.

Mastering the Inner Critic

"Be mindful of negative phrases or voices in your past that replay in your thoughts—some of them work hard to live with you your entire life, adversely affecting your self-image & wounding your self-esteem. Exercise your creativity by creating new phrases that attract positive energy & people to replace anything demeaning. You're the sum total of your deepest thoughts! Be good to yourself every day." — Steven Eric Connor

Let's call the negative phrases Steven Conner mentions in the above passage our inner critic. The inner critic is a mean parent on steroids. It sits on the inside of the mind 24/7, pointing out the evidence it gathers into a smelly mess. Unlike a movie critic, we will never get thumbs up—always two thumbs down—again and again. Sound familiar?

The inner critic likes to make comparisons, and counts what we don't have, what we didn't do, the way we fell short, the way we are still falling short. It bases its opinion on comparing, judging and setting up rules that are unreasonable. Left unchecked, we face a mind lashing every day. No wonder we find a need to medicate this nagging voice.

The inner critic can serve a purpose, and if we learn to come to terms with it (send it out for milk and cookies once in awhile), we can find peace of mind. Sometimes, when my critic gets too loud, I talk to it, "Thank you for your comments. I know you're watching out for me. I am grateful. Yes, I can always be better, but I'm not comparing myself to anyone else. Let's be honest. We can celebrate the fact that I have the guts to try this in the first place. I'm doing OK, don't you agree? I'm a grown up and I'll be fine right here."

Spiritual Advisor Rev. Cynthia Williams gave me another effective way to fill the void of the negative thoughts. Monitor each negative thought by "flipping it" with a positive thought. For example, when "I'm not attractive" comes up, immediately replace it with, "I have great eyes," "I love my smile today." Make yourself do it at first, and then form the habit. When we begin to count what we have, we will be overwhelmed with what we take for granted. We begin to notice and appreciate our hot running water, comfortable bed, caring friends, loving pets...on and on, we count our blessings.

ROCK SOLID CONFIDENCE

24

CHAPTER 4

MASTERY OVER JEALOUSY

*"Wisdom too often never comes, and so one ought
not to reject it merely because it comes too late."*
— Felix Frankfurter, Supreme Court Justice

It doesn't matter what we call it: competition, sibling rivalry, professional jealousy, suspicion, resentment— mastering this ugly feeling will set us free. Jealousy is one of the main issues related to confidence because when we are jealous of another, we project outside ourselves what we don't have rather than looking at all the gifts we do have. The more we focus on others, the more power we give away to them.

Any time we feel disempowered, for whatever reason, through looks or through occupation, we tend to push the one we are jealous of away. It's important to know that the people we attract in our lives are like us—or on our level—in some way. *"Birds of a feather flock together,"* the old saying goes. Again, if you have attracted them into your life, then you are on the same level.

Sometimes it gets ridiculous. If a frog shows up with a pretty hat on, we might be jealous because the frog had the hat and we didn't. So it is time for us to get a hold of this insanity and say, "I'm not living my life this way any more because where is the richness in any of this? Where has my life gotten better because of this? It hasn't. It has kept me from having some of the most joyous of all times.

25

How can I be confident in front of an audience, in business or in my personal relationships living with jealousy?"

Jealousy is a thief who robs us of ourselves each and every time. When we rob ourselves, a little of our life force goes. So let's say we feel jealous of the frog with the pretty hat; right then and there we take a chunk of us and give it to the frog. And then there's cute Sally and we give a chunk to her; and then athletic Bob, and we give some to him; and person after person. So tell me, what's left for us?

Jealousy makes us our own worst enemy. So start now calling all those parts back on board. Call all those parts that you've invested in anyone else. Turn your head away from jealousy and say, "I am better than that, I will not accept that anymore. Do you hear me, my mind? I will not accept that anymore." At night when you go to sleep, visualize all those pieces of yourself coming back. And say, "I'm done. I am done. The buck stops here." It must stop here or there's no room for you in your own life.

Nothing is more beautiful than you. If our Creator had wanted 1,000 different Angelina Jolies, He would have put them here. If He didn't want YOU to be your authentic self, you would have been a clone of someone else.

But you see, dear reader, you are unique. You have a template and a mission that no one else has. No one can duplicate what you came here to do, but you won't get it done if you think everybody else is better. Because you haven't valued yourself and your mission. And this is a part of your *Rock Solid Confidence*.

How long does it take to master jealousy? Anything can be solved in a moment. It's all about us disciplining our thoughts. Perhaps it's like mastery of any skill. We work at it faithfully each day and little by little, what we desire comes to us.

On a personal note, in the past, when I had negative thoughts or bad feelings about someone, I'd sit down and think about the situation. Attempting to solve the problem with logic seemed to be, well, the logical thing to do. However, my mind and my inner critic ganged up on me—took me off on a tangent. And somewhere way down the road, after I'd beat myself up enough, I would come back to my senses, but by then I was exhausted. So now, I handle it immediately.

What I learned to do when jealousy, fear or any other negative emotion comes on my radar screen is to see a big red X over the thought and say, "cancel, cancel." It may sound silly, but after trying it for a couple of days, I realized that it was so much easier than bringing the thought in for examination. Pretty soon the mind is trained to put an X in front of any negative thought the second it comes in; and then flip the thought to what we *do* have. Try it. You might say something like this:

"I will not accept this. I am a beautiful person. I see the many gifts I have. I choose to believe in me. I have a mission to do that nobody else can do. I am determined to do it!"

Stamp out jealousy—no matter how it shows up in your life—and you'll discover a new sense of freedom.

ROCK SOLID CONFIDENCE

CHAPTER 5
HAVE YOU MEMORIZED YOUR SCRIPT?

All the world's a stage;
And all the men and women merely players.
They have their exits and their entrances;
And one man in his time plays many parts.
 — William Shakespeare's *As You Like It*

If we are all actors on a stage, as Shakespeare suggests, then we have lines to learn and we've learned them well— sometimes too well. Our lines come from scripts given to us long ago. It doesn't matter where we picked them up, it just matters that we recognize them as poorly written, outdated and untrue.

Common scripts are:

- I'm not beautiful
- I'm dull and not very smart
- I have bad luck
- No one can love me
- The good stuff comes to everyone but me

Humor is a great way to master negative scripts. Visualize your life as a stage play. You're on the stage going about your daily routine, when someone or something begins to trigger you. Look up, stage left. There in the balcony are three friends laughing at the silliness of your dilemma. In between their belly laughs, they say, "Is he really going to take *this* seriously, again?" And since they're not really laughing at *you* but at your *usual response* to the high dramas of your life, you smile back, thus defusing the charge.

Just as laughter makes everything better, the thought of laughter reminds us that life challenges us to give our best performance; we are tested each day. We need to stay present and choose a new response to an old scenario. Now look back at the balcony, to see those friends applaud another step in mastering the journey.

An affirmation is a 180-degree flip in thinking. Unlike the inner critic, the affirmation is a statement that we repeat to ourselves until the message sinks in. We don't really have to believe what we say to make it work.

Much has been said about the potency of affirmations. There is power in words, and when we are busy saying positive and uplifting things about ourselves, we replace the negative scripts. If jealousy arises, we can say, "Alright, here it is again. I can see it. I can feel it. What part of me is looking outside rather than inside?" At that moment, bring all thoughts and appreciation back to the self—and smile! The balcony gives us a standing ovation!

For a Toastmasters speech contest one year, I chose the topic, "I can't cook." I affirmed the topic during my many practices, and soon, to my surprise and at my family's expense, I began to burn the meat, get more deli foods and in general, lose confidence in my cooking abilities. That fateful speech was just an exaggerated story in an attempt to be funny, but pretty soon my story became my reality.

An affirmation is a new perspective, a new script—a new story we tell ourselves.

- *I can't cook* is now: I ENJOY COOKING NOURISH-ING MEALS.
- *I'm not beautiful* becomes: I AM BEAUTY.
- *I'm dull and not very smart* changes to: I HAVE MANY TALENTS.
- *I have bad luck* is now: GOOD THINGS HAPPEN TO ME EACH DAY.
- *No one can love me* is: I LOVE AND CHERISH MYSELF.
- *The good stuff comes to everyone but me* becomes: I AM ENJOYING MY HEART'S DESIRE.

There are many books about affirmations for your further study. Arlene Rosenberg's book, *Say It, See It, Be It: How Visions & Affirmations Will Change Your Life* is just one example of how affirmations are becoming a popular topic for both business and personal goal setting.

My presentation clients find some audiences more difficult to work with than others. Below is a list of the audience types and an affirmation to help them rewrite their scripts.

Groups of Men:
"I enjoy speaking with men. The logical and practical side of this audience is refreshing. They offer me a delightful change of pace and stimulate my natural sense of curiosity."

Superiors or those with more education or more specialized training:
"I am happy to be around people who have goals and ambitions, much like my own. The differences in life experiences make for a great exchange of ideas. I bring my perspective and life experiences, and I honor their

knowledge and experiences. Speaking with them will be mutually beneficial."

Peers:
"I am delighted to speak with those who have chosen a similar career. Despite any surface feelings, we help each other and support each other. I give my best to each situation and trust that they will do the same. I honor each person here today and celebrate our association.

Audiences with no outward response to you/your message:
"I am here to give my gift of information to these people. They are free to think, feel and respond in a manner that is appropriate for them. My energy comes from my heart, my soul, my core. I am confident that I am bringing my best to them. Long term change rather than an immediate positive response is what I intend to create."

Presenting yourself with assurance requires freedom from the gravity of negativity. It all starts with knowing who you are and speaking the language of your audience to get the results you desire. In the next chapters, we'll examine who you are and what you bring to the stage of *your life*.

Part 2
ROCK SOLID YOU

"This above all, to thine own self be true, and it
must follow as the night the day thou canst
not then be false to any man."

WILLIAM SHAKESPEARE IN *HAMLET*

Rock Solid Confidence

CHAPTER 6

YOUR PERSONAL JAZ^{SM}

"Always, as you travel,
assimilate the sounds
and sights of the world."
— Walt Disney

This is the most important part in the book. Make sure you have a journal to write notes about yourself, because you, dear reader, have the power to change the world. I don't have your exact assignment in front of me, so let's just call it your Personal JAZ^{sm}. Whatever your life's purpose, you will not be able to accomplish your good intentions without the backbone it takes to be you, no matter what others think, no matter what happens to you.

Years ago, in Iowa, I developed a program called "Character Safari" where we trained teens to present to younger students. The goal was to share with younger students the lessons they had learned, thus leaving a legacy. The specific character traits varied and yet the message was the same: the secret to your high school success is to have the courage to make your own choices. Students who were active in extra curricular activities and other leaders were chosen to be "safari guides." The most surprising thing to me was the initial inability of the students to articulate what made them successful, which became the focus of the training.

One of my favorite examples is the homecoming king, a charming young man, Darin, with brown eyes and a ready smile, who was not able to decide on a topic. During our discussion, Darin admitted that in the sixth grade, he was chubby with no friends. It became immediately obvious that his story was how he transformed from no friends to homecoming king. When he presented to his peers, they sat on the edge of their seats. I listened, too—we're all looking for the secret to be loved!

So I ask you to do the same. What are your secrets for success? Perhaps they are hidden even from you, and certainly many of us have an idea that we have some valuable commodity lurking somewhere inside, but we have been told not to brag. So our suspected greatness remains hidden away. It's like having money in several banks. You might be rich, but if you don't know which banks or which accounts, you cannot access your wealth. Your Personal JAZ^{sm} is your personal wealth.

For this reason, the first stop of our journey is self-assessment. What do you have to work with? Most people will be able to make a long list of faults and ways they disappoint themselves. Looking at what's wrong is a shallow self-assessment, filled with judgment. It is a rare client who is able to name, with realistic honesty, the ways they shine—the bouquet of gifts, talents and experiences that make them unique. How can you "bring it" if you don't know what "it" you have to bring?

After all, if you are a salesperson, they're buying you. If you are a speaker, they are buying you. If you are an artist, minister—it doesn't matter—the influence of the human factor cannot be overemphasized. As Roger Ailes' book title so aptly tells us, *You are the Message.*

A limiting thought might be an old script that says, "If I love myself too much, I'm not open to love anyone else and so how can they love me back?" This is an ugly rumor and is completely false. The more you love yourself, the more capacity you build within yourself to love others. We teach people how to treat us, and if we are overflowing with love, we light up and become more attractive. This concept will be mentioned again, so if it is not within your current belief system, try it on gently.

This is the chocolate sundae portion of the book. It's all about you! We'll explore modes, skills, values and in the end, you'll be able to itemize your greatness. Don't feel as if this is an exercise in being self-absorbed, you're just getting clear about you. The next chapter will give us the next step in relating with an audience. For now, focus on *you* in your raw, unencumbered beauty. Get a journal or a notebook and start your list.

Each item represents a rock, a piece of the backbone of your confidence. All presentations and encounters are built with full awareness of this backbone. That's how vital this chapter is to your development. When teaching or coaching, I never skip this step, even if it seems to have no purpose. Let's begin with four modes of communication. I call them: Organizer, Action Hero, Team Builder, and Creator.

FOUR MODES OF COMMUNICATION

Life is a balance of conflicting and harmonious pieces of a puzzle. Below is a set of four words that are both similar and opposite. The Organizer and the Creator are one pair and the Action Hero and Team Builder are the second pair. Like opposite ends of a continuum, neither is better or worse, but all are necessary aspects of our human nature. In order to consider their unique qualities, we'll speak of them in their extreme forms during this initial reading. Later in the book, we'll evaluate how their conflicting and harmonious aspects are used by successful people.

Organizer

Consider the degree to which you organize. The Organizer places things in a sequence and finds a pattern. Attention to details, analysis and long deliberations are important. Someone who is especially strong in this area makes decisions like a judge—over-night based upon research and data. Like flour in a cake, the Organizer represents the substance of an issue.

Visually we see neutral colors, caution, reflective thought, and reserved conservative behavior. When we listen, we hear specific details, serious tones, continuous sound, with little voice inflection and critical analysis. Telling the truth involves the exact truth: "The fish was 6.247 inches long."

The Organizer is great for checking her facts, being calm in a crisis, and making well-researched decisions. She provides the steady, stable anchor, and is the one who devises a flow chart and a plan.

Of course, there is a down side when using only the organizer side of our personalities. When taken to extreme, the Organizer will lack spontaneity, be a bit rigid, feel frustrated about not reaching perfection and often tell too many details that don't connect with the audience.

Organizer types have blessed my life by their detailed instructions (including exactly when to get in the left lane) in getting through Minneapolis. One engineer helped me with my bid for his ham radio convention. He noticed a tiny inconsistency in my presentation book, "You said 14 feet on page 3 and 15 feet on page 9, which is it?" When approaching the overwhelming task of disposing and distributing items from our parents' estate, one of my sisters created a system to organize and disperse much of what was there. Where would we be without the Organizers of the world?

In your journal or notebook, list words that describe your Organizer side. Focus on the positive, but if you do see something that could use improvement, make a separate list and title it, "goals for future improvement."

Action Hero

In many ways, the Action Hero is opposite the Organizer, however, they are both task-oriented. The Action Hero is more concerned with winning and losing, the bottom line, big picture results, and being decisive. He makes a great umpire where quick and accurate decisions are the name of the game.

As you might guess, the truth to him is a direct sort of honesty with no punches pulled, and sometimes he is surprised when his honesty causes hurt feelings. "I was just telling you the truth. Didn't you just ask me for my opinion?"

As a cake ingredient, he is the baking powder that causes movement and action. Many traditional coaches, bosses and "just do it" people use Action Hero skills. We see powerful colors, firm gestures, confident posture, impatient toe tapping. We hear advice, short phrases, big picture messages, urgency, and opinions that sound as if they come from the voice of God.

If you are a strong Action Hero, then you bring a sense of confidence with you, have typically been placed in leadership roles, and are able to get to the heart of the matter in many settings. When taken to extreme, the Action Hero does not value/hear the opinions of others in the group, steps on toes without awareness, and is mistakenly accused of not caring for people.

One Action Hero I admire was quick to take action when a neighbor died suddenly. This person stepped up to the plate, uninvited and without apology, to give each neighbor a job to do. Another led his team into the jungle, and still another made her sales calls with no thoughts of rejection when someone was rude. We depend upon Action Heroes to get things done in the world.

In your journal, record all the ways you shine as an Action Hero. Be sure to save any negative observations for the second "goals" list.

Team Builder

The true opposite of the Action Hero is the Team Builder. I say opposite because of their complementary approaches to life; the strengths of one are the challenges of the other.

The Team Builder's communication goal is to protect and build relationships with others. He truly cares about others and will listen to the details of our stories and support our point of view. He is warm in nature and smiles generously. While the Action Hero is concerned about the success of the task, the Team Builder cares about feelings and asks questions to get a consensus. His voice may be laced with sweet music and his words intend to shelter the esteem of the other. He doesn't like conflict, so to get his honest opinion is a delicate dance. He is the sugar of the cake and just like Meg Ryan in *You've Got Mail*, everything is personal—including business.

We see more pastel colors, smiles, two-handed handshakes, hugs/pats on the back, and nods of approval from this group and we hear questions, compliments, encouragement, heartwarming stories, sincerity and words like "together," "friends," "relating" and "bonding."

The Team Builder is vital in a cold world because he adds charm and grace. Where there is a Team Builder, we have someone to hear and accept us unconditionally, nurture our gifts and provide safety. At times, this group is looked upon as weak; questions are misunderstood for questioning and if boundaries are not established, the self can get lost in the quest of building the team, a friendship or a marriage.

When coming into work, we've all experienced the Team Builder whose sincere "Good morning! How are you?" is filled with hospitality. The refreshing leadership style of the Team Builder honors everyone, and moves the group to a congenial agreement. If the Action Hero boss has stepped on toes, the Team Builder is quick to sense what is wrong and mediate a diplomatic approach to bring peace to the group.

What will you write in your notebook about the Team Builder skills you possess? Make sure you count any actions that go unnoticed by others.

Creator

Last and certainly not least is the Creator, who is the true opposite of the Organizer. This mode shares the "me" focus with the Action Hero and the "people" focus with the Team Builder—but with a touch of spice!

The Creator celebrates unique ideas and spontaneous fun. She can be described as dynamic, electric, engaging, and charismatic. A common phrase in our culture is "coloring outside the box." Yet she does not see a box. Her voice is filled with exclamation points and the truth is the "dramatic truth" rather than the actual truth. "The fish was *THIS* big!"

We see attention-getting colors and textures/patterns, latest fashion/fads, interesting accessories/ties, and sparks of energy. We hear dramatic expressions and words like "fun," "new," "different," "the latest and greatest." She challenges rules and questions authority. She may be an entrepreneur because she has the ability to visualize something that has not yet been created.

If you have many of these skills, your flexibility and spicy personality will win over an audience. However, when used in excess, like salt, too much is not a good thing. Too

41

much can be: too many ideas, too many projects in the works, too many commitments and not enough follow-up on any one of these wonderful creations.

During a seminar, a woman said, "We must take special care to show appreciation for the Creators among us. They are the ones who keep our spirits high and our imaginations active." I agree. It's so fun to hear our Creator friends recall their weekend adventures, and when a wildly fun event is suggested, who can say no?

As you make your fourth journal entry listing your Creator gifts, notice and celebrate the traits in each category. Chances are, you have many more items on the list than you thought. If you don't, go back through this section of the book and take more time reflecting upon your life. All the skills and talents on your list create the sense of balance and harmony necessary to present yourself in public.

BLENDING THE FOUR MODES

Palgwe
Palgwe is descriptive of a world
made up of elements which are both
conflicting and harmonious, i.e.,
sky and earth, light and dark,
man and woman, good and evil.
These elements meet and depart from one another
according to the rules of nature,
thus everlastingly growing and developing.
— Definition given to us by Master David Bruce in
our Taekwondo class

The better you know yourself, the more categories you will place yourself in. A normal healthy person needs all of the skills. Some are natural and feel second nature, while others are the result of practice, habit and perseverance. When someone tells a Creator he is organized, the Creator is pleased to know that his hard work is being recognized! It is fascinating to witness the unlimited shades of diversity possible by combining the four modes. Here are examples of how the modes can be observed in the real world.

- Nancy purchased an office space in a residential area. When she went before the zoning board, this high Creator (C) woman needed to bring out the Team Builder (TB) in her voice when speaking about the situation that led to the owner's need to sell the home. When it was time to show her plans for the business, she gave Organizer (O) details with an Action Hero (AH) tone of voice. Thus she established herself as kind, credible and a woman who can accomplish goals.

- Terry is a family man who builds rapport quickly (TB). He uses his sense of humor (C) to keep clients on the task at hand. The numbers from the client's report (O) establish the point at which his product is most helpful and he asks them to take action (AH) to avoid further problems.

- For her own business, Samantha writes clever copy (C) to market through social networking. Meetings with her are focused (AH) and she'll make recommendations based upon the statistics (O) that are collected from her clients' websites. Many of her connections are based upon her ability to form groups with like-minded women (TB).

- Andrew shows great love (TB) for his family by helping them move (AH) around the country and visits other family members in the process (C). He enjoys his job in the technology field (O) and on holidays, he is most likely to send a "Happy Holidays" text (O) (TB).

- Karen manages (AH) a children's symphony in Houston, Texas. She networks with private instructors, schools (TB) and students, letting them know about the amazing benefits of her organization (C). She coordinates gigs (O) and calms nerves, making everyone feel special and unique (TB).

If you think about those you know and admire, you will observe them blending these four modes as harmoniously as if they were mixing a fine soufflé. Use the examples you see around you to create your own magic recipe *of you*.

Before you begin the next section, ask yourself which is most natural: Organizer, Action Hero, Team Builder, or Creator. Can you see how each mode works in tandem to create balance and harmony in your life?

The four modes will be discussed throughout this book because they have been a foundational part of my work. Even so, there are other ways to describe you, so stay tuned as we explore sixteen speaking skills and other talents you use in your formal and informal communications.

CHAPTER 7
DISCOVERING YOUR STYLE

*"I was never a victim of the times I lived in. In fact,
I was a success because of the times I lived in.
My style of personality became the style.
I was sort of the new woman at a very early point."*
—Katharine Hepburn

Have you ever wondered why we are drawn to some speakers, while others (even though they are doing everything correctly by all commonly held standards) don't hold our interest and attention? In the 1990s I was in three service clubs and served as a Trustee for Kirkwood Community College—all in all, I listened to thousands of talks, speeches, demonstrations and testimonials. During that period of my life it became my hobby to observe the speakers. I saw them break traditional presentation rules and still get rave reviews. How could this be and why were audiences responding this way?

I began to formulate a list of the *exact skills and techniques* that engage audiences. You could say that I became a professional listener. I found everyone to be different: some used many skills while others were strong in only one or two. The common thread: they presented themselves from an authentic, organic place. This is my list and like sixteen shining stars, these skills light up the stage, the board room and the table at the coffee house.

1) Your Smile

The most overlooked skill of all is the smile. What is in a smile? The most obvious part of the face that smiles is the mouth with the turned up line. However, the whole face is engaged when you smile; and I challenge you to observe people in your everyday life as they tell a story or talk about their weekend adventures. What parts of the face are involved? Look at the way their eyes light up, their heads move, their eyebrows change shapes, dimples become vivid and those lovely lines in the face transform. The smile does many things: makes people feel welcome, shows approval, puts others at ease, encourages conversation, and is a personal gauge of what's going on inside.

2) Standing tall/sitting taller

Posture is one of the key elements of this book's topic because it starts a confidence chain reaction. Standing and sitting with the shoulders back, weight equally distributed on both feet not only helps us appear younger and more confident, it also lets us breathe properly, think more clearly and be heard with authority.

Take a look at yourself in the mirror and do this positive-negative exercise. First stand with shoulders pulled forward in a slump; next pull them back and down in a relaxed yet erect position. If this is not a natural position for you, it helps to turn your hands so your palms face out. Repeat this two part experiment until you can see what these two postures do for your outward presentation, as well as how they alter your internal feelings of weakness or power.

Voice coach, Dr. Ralph Hillman from Nashville, advises those who are upset or depressed, "Sit up straight!" and it works. When my clients have tried this exercise, they feel as if they have grown inches taller and feel years younger. They are better able to think, because all of their body parts have room to function and many report feeling empowered because they realize that they get to choose how they stand—which in turn brings a plethora of positive results, including more confidence.

3) Eye Contact

Like smiling, looking at those we are speaking with creates an opportunity for the human, high-touch connection. Eye contact, held no longer than 3-4 seconds, shows respect, gives the speaker clues about the audience's perception of the message and boosts our ability to listen.

Professional salespeople know that listening is the prerequisite to speaking, as this group's livelihood depends upon being sensitive to what is going on in the room. Eye contact goes two ways. We make eye contact to see and be seen. The familiar phrase, "The eyes are the windows to the soul," is on point; our eye contact opens the door to reading body language—which holds most of the message and can be more honest than spoken words.

4) Strong, Clear Voice

Do *you* really need a strong voice? You do if you are an advocate for a cause you are passionate about, a mom who wants her children to listen to her, a customer service representative telling what can be done to fix the angry person's problem. Any job and any person we can think of requires a voice with power.

This is one of my pet interests. Years ago, I sat next to a voice coach at a session at the National Speakers Association and found myself admitting, "I don't like my voice." That was the first step in a long journey of falling in love with my own voice and helping others. In the end, I've had two amazing voice coaches: Ralph Hillman, Ph.D., showed me the vocal choices I could access; and Rob Lindsey-Nassif, a musician and playwright, assisted in refining my skills and demonstrated that I can access power in my voice while maintaining my feminine tones. The magic is in finding the perfect blend.

As we progressed through the belts in Taekwondo class, we could always tell when a new student didn't have the fire to break his board. The kyup would sound shallow. Sound is generated within our inner world and projected through the vocal chords to the outer world. All is revealed through that sound. Listen.

Some of us have difficulty in speaking powerfully because our culture or family taught us it was not "good" to be loud. My nephew was raised in Asia, where it is considered brassy to use a certain volume and certainly not desirable to brag about oneself. When it came time for college interviews in the United States, he needed to put those values in perspective. He gave himself permission to turn up the volume and show enthusiasm for his personal success.

Speaking with enough volume for all to hear is an art. As a presenter, it serves to maintain control and entice everyone to stay with you. If those around us can't hear comfortably, they will become frustrated, angry, or simply "check-out" of the discussion. Harmony High School play director, Mr. Bob Rosedahl used to say, "You can learn your lines and say them correctly, but if no one hears you, what good is it?" Finally, I know what you mean, Mr. Rosedahl!

5) Enthusiasm

Enthusiasm is a not easy to grasp. It's like a wind that stirs and shakes calm waters. It is energy. We can recognize it, but we can't put our finger on it. Some don't think it's a desirable trait because their personalities are naturally more sincere.

We experience enthusiasm as urgency, excitement in the face and voice, and bold gestures. This combination stirs both speaker and audience with excitement. Many coaches display this type of behavior during games, as do motivational speakers.

Enthusiasm is passion expressed in the body and it's a natural outpouring and a call to action. In one scene in the movie *Contact*, Jody Foster's character makes a presentation requesting money to fund a project. When those in the room reject her, she passionately states the importance of her work (what does she have to lose?). Her fear of not getting the money for her project woke up her commitment for her work. In the end, she receives the approval only after her outward expression matched her inner passion.

6) Expressive Gestures

Sometimes when beginning speakers use gestures, they focus on what to do with their hands. Yet the whole body talks! For instance, my former seminar partner, Paul Phelan, Jr., is a more effective speaker when he has the freedom to visually illustrate his stories and move spontaneously. Without this freedom, half the fun of the message is lost.

It's been said that gestures are like punctuation marks. Too many stand in the way of good communication and too few make us look boring. Appropriateness based upon setting is also important: fewer in business settings, more with friends. The natural movements of hands, arms and eyes have the power to convey just the right meaning.

7) Sincerity

This is a quiet, steady expression of emotion, related to enthusiasm. Eye contact is more caring, direct and the voice is soothing, the movements more calming. Words come from the heart with a gentle ring.

This is the tone one might use when giving an acceptance speech during an awards ceremony. Those with highly sincere personalities want others to know that they are sincere about their feelings, and as a result, may be misinterpreted. Once, I was making a recording explaining the concept of Personal Jaz^{sm}. When we were finished, the technician asked me, "Is this last part supposed to be *really* sad?" I decided I had overdone the sincerity and needed to throw a little jazz into my voice.

Sincerity can be just as powerful as enthusiasm. There are many situations where giving comfort, speaking about a more somber topic and showing the depth of our emotions calls for this quality. Those who are sincere hold our trust and credibility more easily.

8) Vocal Variety

Variety is the spice of the voice. Vocally, you can transform a dull subject into one that is fascinating and gives life to your conversations. Sameness is the enemy of anyone who desires to persuade, inform or entertain.

Years ago, there was a wonderful history professor whose classes were so popular, they were held in the auditorium. He was an interesting looking man, with a white beard and told story after story. I did notice one thing—his voice was filled with exclamation points, and after awhile, I couldn't remember what he was saying; I quit listening. The excitement was there, but my mind needed a break.

The goal is to encourage the listener to remain attentive and the more fun we become, by varying—rate, pitch, length of words, pauses and intensity—the more audiences will join us in the enjoyment of our message.

9) Appropriate Humor/Sense of Fun

Fun does not mean you have to tell jokes. If you don't tell jokes to friends, don't feel you need to search the joke books for your formal presentation. If you do tell a joke, make it a seamless part of your presentation but don't announce the fact that you will now begin with a joke. If you use humor, weave it throughout your presentation. Some speakers start and end with a joke, but once they get into the body of their talk, their words are all sadly serious.

Most of us are not judged on our humor. Unless we do stand up comedy, the goal is not constant laughter. It only takes a moment to share a one line humorous quote, change your voice, speak a few words with an accent, sing two bars of a song that matches your message, use clever analogies, or even laugh WITH someone in the class/audience when *they* say something funny.

Yes, humor can be risky. If you are in doubt about saying something, don't. Keep it at a 'G' rating and as you are preparing your talk, ask yourself, "Who is the butt of this joke? Am I a part of the group? Could my humor be considered condescending or inappropriate?" There are lots of books to guide you and your funny bone. Laughter is refreshingly welcome. Bring it.

10) Effective Visuals/Exhibits

Types of visuals used in presentations change through time, but the purpose for the visual remains the same: to illustrate your words in a colorful, graphic manner. A picture and a very few words can add immensely to your message, yet the visual is not the presentation. *You are the presentation.* Never forget that fact.

Make sure your visual is readable and understandable with as few words as possible. I've attended presentations where the speaker apologizes to the group, "You probably can't see this but…" Why defeat your purpose by showing something unreadable? Also, in the preparation stage, get everything set up in advance—remember to bring spare parts and Plan B!

One common mistake is to speak "to" the visual rather than the audience; and the second mistake is to stand in front of the visual, creating a distracting shadow. All the guidelines we discussed for eye contact are true in every presentation, so keep the connection between you and your listeners. And if you think about it, you want to keep the bonds of communication open as you speak. This will not happen if they and you can't see each other clearly.

11) Logical Organization
Order is an organic part of our world. As summer becomes fall, evening fades into night, traffic turns left, and Tuesday follows Monday, we observe the sequence of life. The human mind is programmed to expect an order and you will help yourself if you tap into this natural flow of one, two, three.

In France, we were presented with a menu of options: starters, entrée, cheese, and desserts. Our British friend was not happy with the order of the cheese. It was not "right" according to the way he was raised. In any type of presentation or conversation, there are three natural segments. Simply put, there is a "Hello" at the beginning, a "Goodbye" at the end and something in between. If one segment is missing, the audience will sense it and become frustrated.

The classic names for these parts are, of course, introduction, body and conclusion. The introduction serves a double purpose. It lets the audience build trust with the speaker, helps them get used to their voice and style, as well as introduces the topic. The message is held in the body, and the conclusion summarizes what was said and calls the audience to action.

What you might not realize about order is that when you feel prepared, you are better able to visualize success and eliminate worry. It has been said that 50% of nervousness in speaking can be attributed to the feeling of not being prepared or being able to visualize how to present the message. I've seen this over and over: a client comes in with bits and pieces of a presentation and as they put them in order, fear turns into anticipation.

12) Interesting Topics

What subjects are interesting to an audience? That depends upon who they are and why they have gathered. Audiences like to receive what has been promised to them in the flier, brochure or introduction. They like to learn something new, have fun or at least be engaged, and they will catch your passion for a topic they've never considered before.

In a business setting, your subject has usually been selected for you and so the first person who needs to be convinced that it is a fascinating topic is you! This is your opportunity to make it come alive—or at least get your audience to understand the importance of the topic. *Never, ever say your topic is boring!* Find the vital, interesting parts and be an advocate of your own work.

If you get to choose your topic, then you'll want to think in terms of what you are most passionate about. You probably can see the topic from many different angles, so choose an angle that would interest the audience. *The intersection of your passion and their interest is the goal.* For example, if your topic is cars and you can talk about safety, new models, gas mileage, and history, choose to focus on safety features if speaking with an older more conservative group and new models with teenagers who would most likely rather look cool than be safe.

A final note. Sometimes it's not the topic, it's the speaker. We all know people who would captivate us by reading the telephone book. Intend to be that speaker!

13) Positive Words/Praise

Using positive words is an attitude rather than a skill; however, it can be a habit we acquire. We enjoy up-beat people who look for the best side of any person or situation. Our everyday work world can be a desert with little to nourish the soul.

In a recent discussion with Sharon Foster, Ph.D., an educator from Phoenix, it was mentioned that politics is a two-sided coin. In her optimism, she said, "I'm on both sides of the coin. Tails, because there's a building on that side, and I'm all about building; and heads because when your head is up, you're seeing the bright side of the situation."

There are many presenters who forget to mention colleagues, supervisors, and others who have been instrumental in their work. Once, when a man spoke, giving credit to his wife, I remember feeling better about him. His heartfelt comments uncovered his softer, more caring side. Sincere praise of ANYONE is refreshing and a much needed change in our world. Be sure to use it to leverage your time in the spotlight.

14) Confidence

In his role as a sales manager, Steven Eric Connor uses the word *posturing* when showing a new salesperson the best way to visit a business. The students of Virtuosi of Houston Chamber Orchestra summer camp learn proper *deportment,* so they are ready to look and act the part of a young professional musician. Whether we call it posturing, deportment, or any other word, it's the bravado one needs to approach others with ready anticipation.

We can hear and see confidence by using some of the skills listed in this section. Confidence is the self-assurance and boldness we posses to make decisions, take risks, ask for what we want, feel sure of what we're doing and live with zest. Fifty percent of confidence in a presentation comes from being prepared. The rest comes from experience and trusting oneself. On the deepest levels, it is self-mastery over doubts and fears which is a part of our human experience.

15) Flexibility

The flexible presenter is able to adjust their presentation to the audience as well as the time frame given. Flexibility is a welcome skill as the unexpected happens and the 60 minute time slot shrinks to 40 minutes, electrical problems arise, or a company's sudden downsizing changes the mood of the participants. The more you are present with the total program of the day, the easier it is to be a team member with the meeting planner.

It is hard to state the type of situations you might face, be it challenging people in the room, or unusual physical conditions—any number of issues may arise. Sales people often face clients who insist on leading the presentation. Confidence shows in the poise you have in yourself and allows you to handle any situation with ease and grace. The exact words you prepare are not as important as the spirit of agility you bring to the event.

16) Style

This five letter word is the sum total of who you are and what you do as a person and a presenter. It's what I call your Personal JAZ^{sm}. It refers to all the unique ways you become *you*. When the radio begins to play a Barbara Streisand, Carlos Santana or Kenny G recording, it only takes a few notes to recognize their distinctive flair.

Style takes time to develop, yet by repeating what works for you after a few presentations, eventually, your style emerges. It's the way you bundle all your skills to make you unique. In bowling, we all take the same three steps and throw the ball down the same lane, yet we all look different when we do it.

Communication consultant Roger Ailes says, "The style that's acceptable on television—relaxed, informal, crisp, and entertaining—has become the modern standard for an effective communicator." If you don't feel you have a style of your own, watch movies, observe speakers, politicians, ministers—anyone who is in front of an audience on a regular basis. What are they doing? Imitate. Try on. Whatever catches your eye (or ear) might become a part of your own Personal JAZ[sm].

A Spectrum of Style

The following chart gives a continuum of a few characteristics of style. The middle two words in the chart are the most desirable qualities while the outer words represent going too far. For instance, you can present an idea formally or informally—depending upon what is appropriate for the occasion. If you are too informal, you'll be viewed by your audience as lax; and if you become too formal, you'll be seen as rigid. It's best to keep a happy medium.

(slack, lax)	INFORMAL	FORMAL	(stiff, rigid)
(evasive)	INDIRECT	DIRECT	(blunt, cruel)
(unstable)	EMOTIONAL	LOGICAL	(cold, mechanical)
(scattered)	SUBJECTIVE	OBJECTIVE	(detached)
(exposed)	PERSONAL	IMPERSONAL	(a stone wall)
(crude)	HUMOROUS	SERIOUS	(grave)

In any of the sixteen skills, there are many choices along the way. Make sure you have recorded your strongest skills in your journal. If you don't know, ask a friend. Remember, you don't need to be fluent in all sixteen. Be bold in using what works for you.

TALENT SEARCH

Just for fun, choose words that sound like you and give examples where you have used them in your life.

Coping	Tolerating ambiguity
Decisiveness	Assertiveness
Alertness	Creativity
Versatility	Perceptive
Spoken communication	Written communication
Energizing	Interacting
Reading the system	Team building
Leadership	Decision making
Policy and procedures	Analytical problem solving
Goal setting	Commitment to task
Organizing/planning	Courtesy
Integrity	Perseverance
Indomitable spirit	Self-control
Risk taking	Courage
Orderliness	Initiative
Flexibility	Effort
Sense of humor	Common sense
Responsibility	Patience
Friendship	Curiosity
Cooperation	Caring
Teamwork	Respect
Courageous choices	

YOU ARE TRULY YOU

After reading this chapter and itemizing your talents, skills and gifts, you have a clearer idea of who you are and what you bring to the speaking table. It does not matter if you are interacting one-on-one with a new friend, networking in the community, making a sales presentation in the board room, or addressing hundreds in an auditorium, you bring yourself and your JAZ wherever you go.

The power in this chapter may be missed, so I'm going to restate it. In the many years I've worked as a presentation coach, I always run into the group or individual who insists on digging into their weaknesses, or making a list of strengths and weaknesses. My method works best when you focus on your strengths and reserve judgment on your weaknesses. Executive business coach, Logan Loomis is fond of saying, "In order to stamp out the dark, turn on a light." Knowing your strengths lifts you to them. True, you may have a bad habit or two, yet when you are building confidence, when you concentrate on your gifts, your bad habits fade from view.

There is no one like you in the entire world. No one has your mission in life and if you see your own splendor, you are better equipped to carry out and carry on. Congratulations! This is the first, most vital step along the way. And as Shakespeare would say, *"This above all, to thine own self, be true."* Thank you, dear William.

Part 3
WHAT AUDIENCES WANT

"People don't care how much you know
until they know how much you care."

THEODORE ROOSEVELT

CHAPTER 8
BALANCE AND HARMONY

*"Because a large part of live performance
is the energy exchanged between player
and audience, making another person feel
something—sadness, outrage, joy, laughter—
changes the air you breathe. Your words
take on a life that is both you and
your audience. You both participate
in the creation of an experience."*
— Monica Engesser, actor & comedian

Now that we've discussed challenges in confidence and your amazing and unique talents, it's time to consider the needs and expectations of the audience. Wouldn't it be great to always know what audiences want? I'd like to give you a magic formula.

It's not that easy, yet in this chapter, we'll discuss a few of my favorite models. Like a game, we take our best guess based on what we know to be true. It can be quite exciting. Let's begin by exploring the delicate balance of speaker and audience from a model called Y.O.G.A.

THE BALANCE OF Y.O.G.A.
Y.O.G.A. is a formula I created for a Toastmasters International contest speech. I took this seven-minute talk to the District level, but I didn't win the contest. I did win a lifelong way to look at balanced communication, and I found

that this can be used in informal networking situations as well as formal presentations. The letters stand for:

Y – be **Y**ourself
O – focus on **O**thers
G – be **G**entle
A – **A**dd your personality and zest!

The **Y—Being Yourself** is basic to confidence. We will only mention it here since Part 2 explores this subject in great detail. However, I don't think we can over emphasize the importance of knowing who we are, establishing good boundaries and appreciating the many gifts and talents we possess. When we are self-confident, we experience the freedom to *be*.

Now that we are OK with ourselves, the **O—Focus on Others** becomes important. Be sincerely interested in others before and after the presentation. Smile, lean forward, and look at each individual. Be curious about that person; ask questions and respond with interest by using your body and voice. It's not a good idea to judge or use "yes, but…" statements.

The **G—Be Gentle** might seemed a bit un-assertive, but it does describe the tenderness we humans crave. One of my favorite dentists is gentle—and I appreciate that! In speaking, choose safe topics or at least present your controversial topic in a way that is respectful to the audience. Avoid being too personal or negative. If you offend (and it only takes a second to discover this), sincerely say "I apologize" or "forgive me for…" Express your respect with sincerity.

In every aspect of life, **A—Add Your Personality** is the ultimate goal. It's useful to share a personal experience for the purpose of making a point or building rapport. By showing your natural personality, you invite others to do the same.

If you read and participate in activities that are out of your normal area of interest, you expand who you are as a person.

This last step brings us back to the beginning, so rather than being a straight line, **Y.O.G.A** is a never ending circle of relationship building.

VERBALIstening AND verbaLISTENING

Let's take an in-depth look at the speaker-audience connection. Writing and reading are similar to speaking and listening. One difference is that we can write something today and it is read later—later can be an hour, a day, a year or a century. The writer does not have to be present in order for her words to be received. Speaking and listening happen in real time, almost simultaneously.

Verbalistening is a word I created to symbolize this relationship. Effective speakers speak 80% of the time and simultaneously listen 20% of the time. What are the effective speakers hoping to hear? Their listening is a kind of "reading" of the audience's body movements, gestures, and facial expressions. They're creating a dance of communication. At the same time, good listeners listen 80% of the time and speak 20%. And again, they occasionally speak out loud, but mainly speak with their body movements, gestures, and facial expressions. Below is a chart that describes VERBALIstening and verbaLISTENING.

The Speaker		The Listener
VERBALIstening	and	verbaLISTENING
80-20%		20-80%

Those who present the same material in different settings will confirm that the audience is a key partner in their presentation. When a performer thanks their audience for being a good audience, they're quite sincere! It's a team effort.

THE ELEMENTS PYRAMID

"The teacher is a catalyst for learning; an instrument through which knowledge is transmitted. Teaching happens through you, not by you."
— Sang H. Kim

There are three elements in a presentation: You (the speaker) the Audience (no matter the size or situation) and the Message (topic). There are three ways these elements connect with each other—some are more subtle than others. Since the pyramid is a rock solid structure, we'll use it to illustrate the relationships.

Most obvious, we have the speaker whose job it is to *connect* the audience and the message. You were asked to be the speaker because you have experience or wisdom about the topic. The audience is present because they, too, need or want to know more about what you have to say.

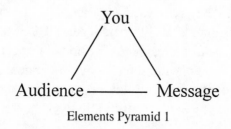

Elements Pyramid 1

In the second pyramid the audience is listening to you to see if you have the *authority* to speak about the topic. Can they respect you? As they listen, they may be asking, "Does he know this topic as well or better than I do?" "What can I learn that will be useful?" Audience members don't need to agree with your point of view; your experiences with the message may serve to expand their thinking.

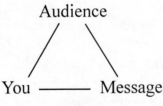

Elements Pyramid 2

A third way to view this pyramid is when the message binds speaker and audience together. Have you ever noticed when audience members become engaged and want to add their knowledge, or will wait in line to talk to the speaker? In this model, *rapport* and synergy are created through the common bond of the message. It's fabulous when respect and learning are reciprocal.

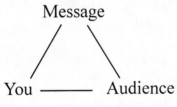

Elements Pyramid 3

The fourth pyramid is an inverted structure that aligns with the beliefs of servant-leadership, a term coined by the late Robert Greenleaf, an AT&T executive. You, as speaker, take the leadership responsibility of bringing the message to the audience in the most ethical manner possible. This model expresses reverence and a deeper sense of care and concern for all involved.

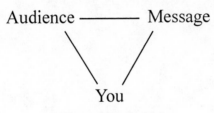

Elements Pyramid 4

All models shown in this chapter illustrate that it's not a good idea to present a canned speech in a vacuum. Speakers and salespeople who are successful shape their prepared remarks around the audience and speaking situation. They realize that no set of words fits all. Presenting well encompasses many factors, and yet when we allow our purpose to guide us, the right words emerge.

Chapter 9
Four Modes—
The Audience Point of View

"If one is master of one thing and understands one thing well, one has at the same time insight into and understanding of many things."
— Vincent Van Gogh.

The best presentations are delivered with the needs and expectations of the audience in mind. In chapter 6, we isolated the four modes of communication in order to understand their differences. However, in this chapter, we will view them in a less stereotypical manner because in truth, audiences have many expectations. They will be mentioned as general categories because we all have a need for order, action, team (or community) and creativity.

When planning your presentation, you'll want to include each of the four modes, yet be flexible in varying the degree of emphasis, based upon the type of audience. Since it is impossible to interview the group before speaking, think in generalities in order to act on your best guess.

For example, when preparing to speak to the Rockwell International engineers, make sure the element of order is present. Yes, it will be important to build rapport, be direct and confident, and put color in the visuals. However, they will appreciate the accuracy of your facts, knowing the source of your research and the logical flow of your concepts more than anything else you do—and if that expectation is not met, you have missed the mark with this group.

As a general guideline, add a healthy mode-dose for these groups and others sharing similar qualities:

Order — engineers, technicians, IT specialists
Action — coaches, CEO's, doctors
Team — teachers, nurses, social workers
Creativity — salespeople, artists, designers

Below are specific suggestions to consider for your next presentation.

ORDER (THE ORGANIZER)

"The first 10 words are worth more than the next 10,000. The last thing you say is the first thing they'll remember." — Kenneth Wydro from *Think on Your Feet*

Order is important in our lives and in our presentations. Audiences vary, but there are organizational elements to check when you plan your talk for all audiences. After putting together your outline, check for: data, facts, concrete suggestions, processes, research, dependable and reliable information and facts presented in a logical sequence. From this list of suggestions, you may want to choose one or two that seem most comfortable and appropriate for your group.

Four Modes—The Audience Point of View

What do High Organizer Groups Expect?

They want respect and understanding. They'd love to see a hard copy agenda, stated objectives, clear directions, and enough time to think and respond. They don't like a speaker who bounces from subject to subject, but rather topics presented logically and sequentially. They also prefer to have material presented in a matter-of-fact manner.

If you are naturally bubbly with dynamic gestures, keep your style, but tone it down, and your message, and you, will be received with a higher degree of credibility. If your style is somewhat subdued, you'll do just fine—yet remember that you are the leader and your passion for the topic needs to be brought forth.

Your goal is to organize your message in such a way that you accomplish the task in the allotted time period. This way, time and energy will be used efficiently and your goals and purpose will be accomplished.

As the speaker, you are in a leadership role; so make sure to remind the Organizers of their value to the organization. It has been my experience that they strive for perfection—sometimes an impossible goal. Their attention to detail in a chaotic world is responsible for the major advancements in technology, science and other fields.

Outlines Create Order

Albert Einstein said," Everything should be made as simple as possible, but not simpler." The following are some of my favorite outlines. The first is a classic speech outline "menu" that can be used as a template for most presentations.

Classic Speech Outline
"Menu"

Introduction
Hello, Appreciation
Story, Quote, State problem to gain interest/see need
Tell what you are going to tell them

Body
Use an organizational structure that fits the situation
Keep message alive with visuals/case studies/physical
objects
(Keep this part flexible to stay within time limits)

Conclusion
Give a summary—specific or general
Ask or tell what you want them to do—call to action

Q&A
Final planned parting words
Words of appreciation

ORGANIZATIONAL STRUCTURES FOR
THE BODY OF YOUR PRESENTATION

These structures can be used as the backbone of your presentation. They are suggestions to get you started when you don't know how to transform your many ideas into a presentation. First, you'll see the name of the model, then the description, a simple example for an imaginary talk, and finally a note about its use.

Q/AAA (Question, Answer, Answer, Answer)
TOPIC: Personal views on the grandparent adventure.

Q: What is it like to be a Grandparent?
A: It is an event that brings back memories.
A: There are privileges yet not as many responsibilities.
A: There is joy in knowing the next generation.

Note: One question has been answered three different ways. This structure can be expanded to any length by adding stories and examples. If you like to make outlines, simply add sub-points or a list of items to talk about after each question.

Q/A Q/A Q/A (Question-Answer, Question-Answer, Question-Answer)
TOPIC: Seasonal traditions

Q: What are common foods for a traditional Thanksgiving feast?
A: Most generally, a traditional Thanksgiving feast would include: turkey, dressing....

Q: What special traditions do you observe during the winter months?
A: Our family is from the north, so we always build snowmen and don't forget the....

Q: How do individuals cope with the post-holiday blues?
A: While it's fun to celebrate each fall, when January comes rolling around many ....

Note: When preparing your talk using this model, ask yourself the questions your audience might have and then arrange them in a logical sequence. Your answer can be as long or short as time allows. As you are delivering the talk, you do not need to ask the question; you may skip this part. Instead use a transition sentence and go right into the next topic.

One year, I wrote my Christmas letter by asking and answering questions about my year. Before printing the letter, I decided to erase all the questions, and the writing flowed without them. Can you see the similarity of organizing for writing and for a presentation?

S/P (Statement, Proof) or
S/PPP (Statement, Proof, Proof, Proof)
TOPIC: Good Pets

S: Dogs make good pets.
P: A dog's loyalty is unwavering 365 days a year.

S: Cats make good pets.
P: They don't need to be walked.
P: Cats have an independent nature and don't need to be entertained.
P: They can take care of their own needs, so they can be left for a weekend.

Note: This Structure is similar to Q/A yet evidence is given more directly. Depending on the topic, audience and purpose of the meeting, proof could be presented in the form of charts, graphs, or case studies.

B.E.S.T. (Belief + Example + Specific-Situation = Total)
TOPIC: Living in Arizona

B: I *believe* Arizona is a wonderful state in which to live.
E: For *example*, no matter where you go, there are mountains to enjoy.
S: (*Specifically*) The Papago Mountains look like ancient people to me.

T: The beautiful landscape of Arizona is a joy each day for those who live here.

Note: This structure is like S/P and S/PPP, however each section builds upon the next. The B is a mini thesis statement, the E gives a general category, S allows us to zoom in— name a detail, and T is a summary of what has been said. This can be used when you want to answer a question or when making a short, but organized remark. If you place three sets of BEST together, you have the outline for a simple presentation. Again, the length of your remarks can vary according to the time available.

Time Sequence (past, present, future)
TOPIC: The automobile

Past: The invention of the horseless carriage
Present: Style and features, fuel options, safety
Future: Global teamwork, cooperative transportation, green considerations

Note: Many subjects lend themselves to this structure. The speaker need not begin at the beginning. Some choose to tell about the present, go back to the past to review history and then project the future. Have you noticed this technique in movies? It's effective because it lets us see time from a different perspective.

Topical (1,2,3,4,5)
TOPIC: Walt Disney Company

1. Mickey Mouse
2. Movies
3. Theme Parks

4. Education
5. Animals and Nature
6. Exploration in Space
7. Adventure and History

Notes: Because this form is modular, you are free to select the topics that seem most appropriate for the audience—from the list of possible choices. Normally, you will choose 3-5. Begin and end with the most important information. For example, if you have 4 subtopics, arrange them in this order:

1st - most important subtopic
2nd -third most important subtopic
3rd - fourth most important subtopic
4th - second most important subtopic

With this order, if time is short, you can eliminate a whole segment of your talk without the audience feeling deprived. Too often when time is running out, we hurry through the whole presentation. Better to take a "less is more" posture.

There are many choices to be made when meeting the organizational needs of your audience. When possible, plan early enough so you can have options. Remember that much of the stress in a presentation comes from not being prepared.

"There is a right time for everything: A time to be born, a time to die; a time to plant, a time to harvest; a time to kill, a time to heal; a time to be quiet, a time to speak up. A time for loving, a time for hating; a time for war, a time for peace." (Eccl. 3:1-8)

CHAPTER 10

ACTION (ACTION HERO)

"When I stand before God at the end of my life,
I would hope that I would not have a single
bit of talent left and could say, 'I used
everything you gave me.'"
— Erma Bombeck

The Action Hero part of us likes to be challenged and values pro-activity and productivity. Audiences appreciate the presenter who moves forward and shares information that can be acted upon. They don't like to sit through a formal presentation full of information they already know; so when you speak to them, have your facts and priorities in order.

If you are in sales, you recognize the Action Heroes in the group by the ease in which they interrupt you. Right in the middle of your artfully planned presentation, they ask a bottom line question like, "How much will this cost us?" Sometimes it's a test of your backbone and sometimes they just want to lead.

WHAT DO HIGH ACTION HERO GROUPS EXPECT?

Your goal with this group is to speak in such a way that you win their interest and get them to take action. What they want is respect and understanding. They're willing to listen to you cover the important points, but no more. Express your own confidence through your voice and posture, even if you are not feeling at the top of your game. Give useable facts, rather than knowledge, that affect their bottom line.

Dale Carnegie gives this advice: *"If you are speaking, forget everything but the subject. Never mind what others are thinking of you or your delivery, just forget yourself and go ahead."* Taking action is all about taking a risk. It's fun to be challenged by this group because interacting with them holds you accountable at a higher level and will almost guarantee your own personal and professional growth. More often, we go to great lengths to overprotect ourselves, which only serves to lower our confidence level.

When speaking with a group of Action Heroes, be aware that they probably may not get a lot of praise. If they are leaders, many feel that they are already self-assured and wouldn't care if they were told how much they were appreciated. Not so. The old saying, "It's lonely at the top," reminds us that we all have human needs. Thank them for their leadership and vision, for keeping focus on the goals— whatever is true and appropriate.

"There are no great people; only great challenges that ordinary people are faced by circumstances to meet." — Unknown author

It's important to master your thoughts, words and sentences. Some statements we make are general in nature and some are specific. Consider how these two types of statements can be used.

Taking Action: Using General and Specific Statements

General statements are handy tools. Like a blanket, they cover a broad topic in a few words. They are useful in a variety of situations:

1. They are great to begin a speech or a conversation. *Every three minutes, someone is changing your pass code.* or *This event is amazing.*
2. They serve as an overview of an agenda. *Tonight we will discuss and vote upon the suggestions made at our last meeting.*
3. They answer the question, "What's your point?" *My goal is to uncover what happened so we can move on with assurance.*
4. They may be used as a way to uncover common interests when meeting a new person. *This is a unique setting, don't you think?*
5. They may be used to defuse or avoid a topic. *He expects a lot of everyone.*
6. They give others the opportunity to answer the specifics. *I'd like you each to state your opinion.*
7. This is a great way to close a conversation at a networking event. *It's been great talking with you.* or *Thank you, I've enjoyed getting to know you.*

Specific statements are also useful, when appropriate:

1. They are filled with detailed information. *As long as you asked, there are three groups you might want to call when you're in the Boston area....*
2. They teach. *Let me tell you about Isis, who was able to bring her husband....*
3. When speakers are passionate about a topic, they use them. *It was a great game. First the....*
4. They paint a picture. *We were both on the beach and as we noticed the sun rise....*
5. They allow us to feel, hear, taste and experience the subject. *Sand sprayed my face and as I reached over to pick up the broken bowl....*

Why are we discussing general and specific statements right now? It's important to be able to communicate appropriately; to be able to flex to a variety of groups. The Organizer side of us will appreciate the specific details and the Action Hero side will smile and nod when we can summarize what we have to say. In most cases, you will use a variety of each. It's called speaking the language of the audience.

"You gotta know when to hold'em,
Know when to fold'em,
Know when to walk away,
Know when to run."
— Kenny Rogers

CHAPTER 11

TEAM (TEAM BUILDER)

"When there is not much difference between
your product and that of your competitors,
there had better be a big difference in the way
you deal with people."
— Jim Cathcart

Building a sense of team is a vital part of your communication repertoire. In fact, it's the first order of
business in gaining rapport with the audience or client.
Sometimes this topic is irreverently referred to as a
"soft skill" by people who don't really understand the
significance of this talent.

The truth is, in a world where there are scammers,
crooks and bad guys; we are running out of trust. In a presentation, it's about building solid relationships, making
friends or at least gaining a sense of trust and caring between
speaker and listener.

WHAT DO HIGH TEAM BUILDER GROUPS EXPECT?

When speaking to groups with high Team Builders
present, be sure to include proof that you are aware of the
dynamics of their group and have a solution to enhance
their sense of team, or at the very least, not affect it
negatively. They value and expect you to show them how
your message/product will assist in caring for the needs of
all, accepting others with generosity, and honoring diverse

opinions. They prefer to keep everyone happy, and love situations where compromise is possible for the greater good.

They want respect, understanding and consideration for the group. If you let them know that you recognize their contribution behind the scenes, you'll be one in a million and they will love you for it!

Establishing your sense of integrity early in the communication is vital for acceptance of the rest of your presentation. Create a safe climate for them to ask and answer their questions honestly and diplomatically. Speak well of all, and even when presenting highly technical material, show the benefits and affects on people.

Your goal is to make everyone look good. By doing so, you create a golden opportunity to brag about those who deserve praise, thus earning the trust and respect of those in the group. Remember, members of this group are used to giving praise, and sometimes don't receive well, but secretly hope someone recognizes their contributions. As a speaker, you can serve in this capacity.

> *"Ask not what your country can do for you; ask what you can do for your country."* — John F. Kennedy

TOO DIRECT OR NOT?

The Team Builder wants to help, and never offend, so when wording questions, make sure that they are broad, not direct. Give options and never pin them to the wall. It might seem like a lot of effort, but if you want to know their true feelings, the question needs to be positioned in just the right way. Here are some examples to illustrate what I mean.

Too direct: How do you like my dress?
Better: Did you notice that I bought new dress?

Note: Asking a direct question will get a positive response, no matter how they truly feel. The second question gives more room for an open discussion. From that, you can gauge the true opinion.

Too direct: Why did you tell him about the car accident?
Better: What were your reasons for telling him about the car accident?

Note: Beginning a sentence with the word "why" is confrontational. Yes, it can be used in certain arenas, just be aware. The second sentence is better for unearthing information because it implies that there is logical thought behind the action. Assuming the best is an implied compliment.

Too direct: Did you even think before you gave her the money?
Better: You've done this sort of thing before and I'm sure you have a strategy for the money you gave her. Could you share your thinking with me?

Note: The words "even think" has the echo of "dummy" lurking behind it. The second sentence is better only if true curiosity is behind your words.

Too direct: How much did you pay for that scarf?
Better: The colors of that scarf are rich and vibrant. It looks expensive.
Alternative: I'd like to buy something like that for my sister. What price range do you think I'm looking at?

Note: In our American culture, it is rude to ask about the price, unless you're shopping in a store. While the second sentences are not questions, they often open up the conversation to price and shopping stories. The alternative response gives your motive and will allow you to get the information you seek without directly asking the rude question.

Too direct: Did you read my new book?
Better: What parts of my book made sense to you?

Note: Since a Team Builder personality lives to make others feel good, they would never admit to not reading all or part of your book. The second question gives them a chance to praise you, which they can probably do at some level.

To summarize this important part of the chapter, let's remember that we are all people doing jobs, living in families and doing the best we can. We are living and playing the human experience, and we carry our humanity wherever we go. Never underestimate the importance of what we learned in kindergarten—the ability to get along with the kids on the playground.

CHAPTER 12
CREATIVITY (CREATOR)

*"There are three things to aim at in public
speaking: first, to get into your subject,
then to get your subject into yourself,
and lastly, to get your subject into your hearers."*
— Alexander Gregg

We live in a world that has color and sound and movement. As a presenter, you have the task of presenting to people who watch professionals on television and the movies, who view computer-animated graphics with all the new bells and whistles. Professional and celebrity speakers hire a team of specialists to jazz up their messages. We've become a bit spoiled. The creator side of us wants to be surprised, to look outside the box and experience the new, or at least the same subjects, through new eyes. You, the presenter, can offer that vision.

WHAT DO HIGH CREATOR GROUPS EXPECT?
When presenting to all groups, and especially to those who value the creative side of life, find ways to be eye catching, artistic and out of the ordinary. Those who are Creators can see what has not yet been created and some do not relate to the popular phrase "thinking outside the box" *because they see no box.*

Like the other groups, they want respect and understanding, yet it is especially important to provide them with an enjoyable experience. You can satisfy this need by using clever words, interesting analogies and attractive visuals. Visuals don't need to come from a screen; in fact, a three-dimensional object or toy that fits your theme is a welcome change.

Flexibility in presenting is important—present with the feeling of spontaneity. Be free to change it up and take one of their suggestions, if possible. Participation is better than a lecture. Count both the number of minutes you speak and the amount of time they get to participate. Even if you are an extremely charismatic speaker, they appreciate joining you in some way.

As with the others, you have an opportunity to express your gratitude to this group for adding their *spice* to the world. Some highly creative people dream so far beyond everyone else, their ideas can seem wild and unworkable. Yet they are responsible for opening our minds; and the passion they bring to the workplace, the board room and the family is invaluable. Let them know this.

Advice from a Creator: Never Give a Speech

1. Never give a speech. We, your audience, do not like to think that you have anything canned for us. Instead, make it natural—just talk with us!
2. The pronouns you use change the impact of your message. Count the number of times you say, "I," "me," "my," as well as the number of times you say, "we," "you," "your." We like it if you make your presentation about "us." Two-to-one is a good ratio.
3. Keep your promises. If you say you'll give three reasons, give three. If you say you'll stop at 10:00 am, honor our time by doing so. If presenting at a convention, read the session description from the flier and deliver what is promised, to the best of your ability.

CREATIVITY (CREATOR)

4. Gestures are for the audience. Make them from the audience point of view. When telling a sequence of events, move your hand from THEIR left to right, not yours.
5. Stories that are personal are great IF the connection is made between your story and the audience's story.
6. When you sincerely praise your spouse, all others of that gender are uplifted. The same is true for sons, daughters, moms, dads, grandparents and other special groups.
7. Dress rehearsals are vital for self trust. With a dress rehearsal, it's never your first time.
8. Taking a risk in one area of your life will help you be more confident in other areas as well.
9. We are judged in three ways: The first gatekeeper is visual (what they see), the second is what they hear (your voice), and if you pass those two gates, then your message has a chance of being received.
10. What you say about a person, place or thing tells more about you than the object of your discussion. Take the high road.

Rock Solid Confidence

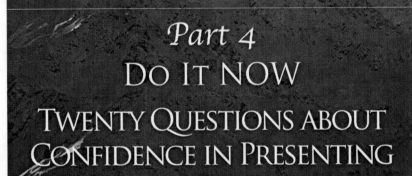

Part 4
Do It NOW
Twenty Questions about Confidence in Presenting

"If it's worth doing, it's worth doing poorly...until you can do it well."

ZIG ZIGLAR

Rock Solid Confidence

CHAPTER 13
CLARITY IN COMMUNICATION

"A spoonful of honey will
catch more flies than a gallon of vinegar."
— Ben Franklin

1) **Someone told me that I should use a mirror when preparing my presentations. Do you agree?**

I'll give you three answers to your question.

I'm imagining that your question has to do with practicing your talk in front of a mirror. Yes, a mirror comes in handy and some speakers use it to watch themselves as they practice. Even better is to use a video camera for practice—to be viewed for your eyes only. In that way, you can separate the role of speaker and listener into two different time periods.

During the recording, you are the speaker. Try different hand gestures, postures, ways to begin and end statements. Then as listener, you have the opportunity to step outside yourself to see *you* as the audience does. You have the chance to know which of those gestures work, which introductory remarks you prefer—in the privacy of your home and in your own time. My clients report looking better than they thought they would. Those jitters that scream at you on the inside are not always as apparent on the outside, and knowing this boosts your confidence level.

Besides the obvious reasons we look in the mirror when we get dressed each day, you may want to look in the mirror for another reason. Look at your face; it is God's creation. Study yourself as if you were a long lost friend. Do this for two minutes each morning; see if you can work up to five minutes. Smile at your beauty. Talk to yourself and agree to let your beauty shine. Don't be alarmed if it is difficult at first. There is no one is the world like you. Cherish that fact!

The third way to think about a mirror is to see those around us as a mirror of how we view the world at that moment. When I feel good, everyone else looks good. When I feel lonely or depressed, I seem to attract that type of person into my life—as if I were a big magnet. Once I became frustrated with my children and shouted, "Quit yelling." Then I realized that I was the yeller, and they were only the mirrors of my mood. If you become aware of strange characters showing up in your life, they are giving you the opportunity to see yourself.

Don't blindly believe anything I say in this book. Test it out for yourself—especially with this last suggestion. Whenever someone you perceive as angry, insincere, or lazy, comes into your life, ask yourself, "What if this person is reflecting something in me? What if their anger, insincerity and laziness are the part of me that I judge?" Work on yourself and see if the actions of others become less important to you.

2) I've been told not to be so negative. I'm not sure what they mean, so how can I change?

Because I don't know you personally, I will give you a good place to begin. Take note of your vocabulary. There are certain words and phrases that bring dark clouds with them. I'll give you a short list. Check your vocabulary for the following phrases:

"Yes but...."

This phrase can be said with all the right intentions if you're a person who wants to look at all sides of the situation. The word "but" brings a change, so each time you use it, you've just cancelled what was said before it. It is better to put your warning in a new sentence: "Yes I'd love to go. Unfortunately, I promised my son I would take care of his dog tonight."

"I don't know..."

Once, I had a client who would answer every question with this phrase—followed by a fantastic answer. First words give first impressions. If you are not 100% sure of your answer, you might offer a limitation or qualify your comment: *"As far as I know*, the temperature is going to be in the low 30s."

"No, we can't do that..."

A general rule is to avoid the word *no* as much as possible. Be thoughtful with this suggestion and say, "It would be fun to go to the movies, yet we don't have the money right now."

"You don't understand..."

Hidden in this sentence is the connotation that the person you are talking with is not smart enough to comprehend what you just said. Communication is a two-way street and if you are explaining an idea, you have a responsibility to speak so they can understand. Better to say, "I apologize for giving you that impression. I intended to tell you that I would be an hour late."

"To be honest with you..."

If you say this, it gives the listener a reason to question other things you say. Shall you be believed all the time, or just when you admit to your honesty? It's better to say, "I usually don't share my personal life, but I've been in therapy for two years."

"Why did you..."

Small children sound innocent when they ask "why" but as adults, it comes with the connotation that we see no thought behind the action. If this is changed to "What were your reasons for..." the conversation has a chance to unfold.

"No problem..."

Although a popular phrase, the main word is negative and heavy. Use a more positive word with a pleasant tone of voice. Anything we say with a judgmental tone will sound negative. Take, for example, the words "fine" and "great." It's better to say, "It will be fun to help you."

Here are a few uplifting words and phrases to add to your vocabulary:

"Certainly..."

Instead of saying, "Ya," "Yes," "Sure," "No problem," the word certainly is surprisingly pleasant to the ear. When we stayed at the Ritz-Carlton in Florida, all the staff used this golden word. "Certainly I'll bring the water without ice."

"As far as we know..."

This phrase allows you to add a qualifier to a bold statement. "The delivery is tomorrow, as far as we know."

"Thank you for..."

When we're appreciative of those around us, negativity fades away. The two just don't mix. Express your gratitude to everyone you meet—it will lift your mood. "Thank you for opening the door for me."

"With your permission..."
These words precede a direct statement, making it charming and cordial. "With your permission, I'll drive your car," "With your permission, I'm giving my gift to your daughter."

"It was my pleasure..."
When you truly mean it, this praise is so much better than "you're welcome." It helps us realize that the giver gets something out of the act of giving. "It was my pleasure to wash your dishes."

You may like some of these suggestions better than others. Try the ones that fit your style best, and realize that you might be a bit awkward at first. Your gracious heart will be your best guide in transforming a negative presence into one of uplifting sincerity.

3) I want to be able to speak louder, avoid mumbling. How?
If you notice that you're asked to repeat what you say quite often, or if you are frequently misunderstood, you'll want to address the volume of your voice. Try these ideas:

1. Stand and sit up straight. It sounds like advice you'd get from your mother or 3rd grade teacher. They were right. Your body was made to function in a fully upright position. Don't forget to breathe deeply! It improves your voice quality and will improve your volume as well.
2. Sometimes you can be heard but the words can not be processed. Give each word or phrase its own space. Listen

to network newscasters. Their words have a cadence—a beat. When speaking to a large crowd, you may have the feeling that you are "walking in mud" with your words. Use an audio or video recorder to test yourself.

3. Create a practice session for yourself where you select a sentence to repeat several times. Speak in a very quiet tone, and then as if you were turning up the dial on the radio, get louder. Imagine going from a 1 to an 8. Record your voice and see how the quality changes with the volume. Determine which level is best for you and if possible, get feedback from someone you trust.

4. Make sure you say the last word of each sentence as loudly as the other words. Chances are, your audience misses your point by missing out on that last key word. Move the front part of your mouth when you speak. This effort alone will slow the pace of your words and enhance your articulation.

5. Picture yourself as a confident speaker with an important message. Practice using a strong voice in everyday situations where you are not being judged: at the post office, grocery store, in traffic. When speaking to a group, let your passion show.

4) I'm not one to give a lot of compliments, because I don't want to appear to be insincere. How do I get started knowing what to say?

I agree that sometimes we don't know what to say when we are faced with a new situation. It's always helpful to plan ahead. My belief is: what you say is a reflection of who YOU are.

Once, I worked for a man who had a reputation for being difficult. When I resigned my position, several people asked me what he was *really* like. I wanted to be truthful, but because of the nature of his work, I wanted to avoid making a negative public comment. My planned answer was, "He puts in a lot of hours and expects the same from his staff." That was the truth and it was enough information to satisfy the general public.

Make a list of those you interact with in business or social settings. After each name, write three adjectives describing each person. Be honest about how you really feel—this is your confidential list. Some of the words might be positive and others more negative in nature.

Now flip the negative descriptions to the positive. For instance, change "stubborn" to "has strong convictions" and "lazy" to "is easy going." Now practice. The next time you see one of these people say, "Tom, I've always admired the way you are able to stay firm in your convictions." And you'll mean it!

Rock Solid Confidence

CHAPTER 14

THE HEART OF CONFIDENCE

"Courage does not always roar.
Sometimes courage is the quiet voice
at the end of the day saying,
'I will try again tomorrow.'"
— Marry Anne Radmacher
from *Courage Does Not Always Roar*, Conari Press

5) I'm faced with extreme anxiety when I speak. What can I do?

Anxiety is more common than you think. Most people I've worked with are fine in one setting but others are problematic—certain people, places and situations feel intimidating. My dad used to say, "I felt like a penny waiting for change."

As an example, consider your foot. You've had it a long time and yet even before birth, it was complete. No matter how old you are, it is 100% formed and complete, even though it has great potential for growth. You and I as presenters are the same. Anxiety gives us the feeling something is missing when really this is not true. With each experience we grow, and there is nothing wrong with us right now.

Take a moment to ask yourself about your anxiety:

Who is my best and worst type of audience?

Are there speaking locations that trigger my anxiety or make me feel uncomfortable?

Which topics are easy/fun and which are especially difficult for me?

When you answer these questions, you arrive at the heart of the matter. This is a very big step in the right direction.

Here are suggestions to build your confidence and shrink your anxiety:

1. Take risks and praise your accomplishments, however small they seem.
2. Practice speaking with friends.
3. Give your opinions to people in "safe," comfortable public settings.
4. Join an organization and begin by giving public compliments to the leaders of the group.
5. When you feel ready, volunteer to hold office where giving a short report is expected.
6. Volunteer to speak in public with a partner. Two are safer than one and with the right partner it can be lots of fun.

6) What can I do to calm my nerves when I get asked to speak?

A certain amount of excitement is good before speaking. At the race track, I want to bet on the horse that is exploding with anticipation of what is to come, rather than the one who is slouching around the track. The same is true of speakers. Audiences prefer a speaker who is excited and takes the engagement seriously.

Having said that, it's not healthy to have deer-in-the-headlights fear.

The following are nine specific suggestions to prepare you to speak with confidence. They help you be mentally prepared. Giving your mind a task keeps it away from creating critical thoughts to sabotage you.

1. **Make a timeline for your presentation.** Decide what needs to be done and stick to your plan.
   a. month before (or more if time allows)
   b. few days before
   c. night before (be good to yourself—make sure you are rested)
   d. presentation day
   e. upon being introduced
   f. during (enjoy!)
   g. right after (don't read your evaluations right now, if possible. You've given all you have and won't see the comments clearly.)
   h. next day (now is the time to consider improvements)

2. **Shine the light on the audience.** If you visualize yourself as the speaker shining a spotlight on members of the audience, it won't occur to you to be nervous.

3. **Be an advocate.** Have you ever noticed that when a speaker is fully committed to a cause, her voice comes from a deeper place and conviction replaces fear? Others hear your confidence and the best news is that you hear yourself in two ways. You hear your voice on the outside and you feel it on the inside. No matter the topic, this double blast of conviction is accessible when you see yourself as an advocate rather than a speech-giver.

4. **Know your purpose/mission.** In planning your talk, state your mission or purpose for giving the presentation. Everything you say should support the mission and become another way to keep your mind busy with productive thoughts.

5. **See yourself accepting any situation with poise.** Know that there might be technological challenges or other unexpected glitches. Anticipate a few and have a Plan B. It will help you feel "ready."

6. **Talk with one friend at a time.** As you speak, choose one or two friendly faces in different sections of the room. If a few don't seem outwardly accepting of your message, don't spend time "winning" their approval—you don't know what is going on in their lives at that moment in time. Focus on those who are giving you encouragement with their body language.

Note: Early in life, I discovered how important it is to smile at a speaker. So if you'd like speakers to give you more personal attention—support their efforts.

7. **Bring in the support of the silent partner.** This suggestion is for the speaker who might say, "What would my Dad say to me if he were here?" Imagine someone from your life or perhaps (if this is in alignment with your beliefs) an angel or other spiritual being. Hear the words they would say to you to encourage you to be *bold* and be your *best self.*

8. **Write and say a positive affirmation.** Affirmations are statements that affirm you. Simple is best: "Yes I can." "I am confident." "I am ready." Positive thoughts and self-talk chase away negative thoughts. Maybe they are effective because they are just a little too perky for those negative thoughts.

9. **Volunteer to speak.** Ease into the speaking game by volunteering to make an introduction or a short statement

at a meeting. Since the spotlight is not on you, the pressure is not as great and no one will know you are building your confidence for larger projects.

These are simple ways to physically calm yourself just before a presentation.

1. Lip balm keeps your top lip from sticking to the roof of your mouth.
2. Breathe deeply as it will relax your body.
3. Tighten muscles, then relax and the contrast will bring you into a deeper state of relaxation.
4. Stand or sit up straight in order to help your body function properly.
5. Keep a cloth handy to dry your hands of perspiration and you'll be a confident hand shaker.
6. Stand behind the lectern at first, and then come out once you feel "safe."
7. Use notes or a script as a crutch. In most cases, it is not necessary to memorize.
8. Present with another person and share the spotlight, responsibility, and nervousness.
9. Impressive visuals act as a partner to take some of the "attention" away from you.
10. Begin by sincerely praising someone in the room—or everyone. Good feelings come back to you with this act of appreciation.
11. Look into the eyes of those listening to you and send gratitude.

7) Do you have any advice for being consistently confident?
     Confidence levels rise and fall for many reasons. When speaking, the goal is to maintain a balance between

being happy to share your important message and being aware of the responsibility for giving something of value to the audience.

We get into trouble when we use the platform or the training room as an opportunity to: judge ourselves against other people, "show–off" our speaking abilities, or vent angry/hurt feelings. Be there to give value to the audience. In other words, when we hold the right intentions, we do just fine.

Preparation will boost your confidence level, so again, I emphasize the importance of organizing your message early. I worked with a client who had been very nervous about giving a talk. Her church members begged her for years— but she declined. She assumed it was fear holding her back, but as soon as a brief outline was set and she "saw" the flow of her presentation, she relaxed.

Be aware of the needs of the audience and feel comfortable with your visuals. It's best to practice your presentation 4-6 times out loud and if possible, get feedback from a video camera or a colleague. As you prepare, avoid those who are overly critical of you, even beloved family members. Sometimes in their enthusiasm to help you be your best, they inadvertently overwhelm you with "flaws" to erase. This is the time to count what you have to give to your audience.

If you are able to practice your presentation or at least stand behind the lectern in the room where you are going to speak—as we saw in *The King's Speech*—you boost your confidence by physically experiencing the exact speaking environment, envisioning the faces who will benefit from your message. This frees you to concentrate on the task at hand.

We are all on a path of growth, so don't expect to be Tom Hanks or Meryl Streep overnight. Expect to be human.

Know that audiences like real speakers. If our intentions are truly for their benefit, they'll forgive our small mistakes. No presentation, training or class is perfect. The best news is—words are like puffs of smoke. They disappear so quickly that if we don't let on we have used incorrect grammar or mispronounced someone's name, most listeners will not notice—unless we tell them!

8) What are some ways to show confidence?

Confidence is a mysterious mix of how we sound and look—like an invisible cloud encircling us. It is easy to tell when someone is not confident. Occasionally, it's helpful to look at the behavior we want to avoid in order to gain clarity on what we wish to achieve.

Participants in a recent Personal JAZ[sm] class identified the following ways NOT to show confidence:

1. Speak with a diminished voice: fast, soft or high pitched.
2. Keep right on talking, ramble aimlessly and don't worry about getting to the point.
3. Slump, slouch and shuffle as you stand before a group.
4. Don't look at anyone's face.
5. Repeat and repeat.
6. Fill all word-less spaces with "ah" and "um" and "annnnnnnnnnnnnnnnnd."
7. Let your hands and shoulders flinch.

They also made a list of traits confident speakers share:

1. The voice is dynamic and powerful.
2. Their speech is like a poem: brief, yet complete.
3. They are comfortable with silence. They don't have a need to fill every second with the sound of their own voices.

4. Eye contact is relaxed and controlled.
5. Gestures are strong but don't distract from their words.
6. We believe them when they speak.
7. They are warm and sincere.
8. Smiles are genuine.
9. Posture is erect, yet natural.
10. They are embracing of others.
11. They choose their words with care.

CHAPTER 15
ENHANCING STYLE

*"I long to accomplish a great and noble task,
but it is my chief duty to accomplish small tasks
as if they were great and noble."*
— Helen Keller

9) People say I am too tough, that I don't care. That's not true. I am responsible for results, not for making everyone feel good.

This is a common concern with people who speak the Action Hero language. You are probably in charge of a project. You are fully committed to this project and have the BIG PICTURE in your head. Your name will most likely be associated with the success or failure of the project. Besides, you have a personal pride and a natural direct nature.

So the real question is, how do you say, "Just do it! Do it because I SAY SO. Don't ask questions. Don't question my sanity or authority. There will be no discussion about this!" without sounding like a military superior, a mom or a second grade teacher?

My suggestion is to address the feelings first, yet be firm in the action to be taken. The following is a list of phrases you might use to accomplish this task. Modify this list—use what fits your personality and situation.

Note: Make certain you don't connect the two parts of your statement with the word "but." After acknowledging their feelings, use "and" or simply start a new sentence.

"But" cancels out what came before and you don't want to accidentally take away from or belittle their feelings.

1. I know this is different from... yet we have a responsibility to...
2. I understand that you are upset about...however my decision is to...
3. This will not be easy... the bottom line is...
4. You may feel... however it has been decided...
5. We are not used to doing it this way... We will comply with the new...
6. I felt ... Now I understand the importance of...
7. I wouldn't blame you if you thought... However, we have a job to do and...

The common thread in all these statements is the way they begin. The message is, "I am aware of your thoughts and point of view. I care about you. I respect you as a person. I hear what you are saying." The person you are dealing with may not fully agree but is more likely to respect you when your words are given in the spirit of honesty and sincerity.

10) How can I show more enthusiasm in my presentations?

We can only be truly enthusiastic about topics we care about. If you are not excited about your topic, you have two choices. Choose another topic or uncover why this topic is important and interesting. In many business settings, topic selection is not up to you, but your perspective is always your choice.

Some of us are passionate about our message, but we don't have a flashy out-there-on-the-edge manner of expressing this feeling. Earlier in this book we talked about both enthusiasm and sincerity. If your style is more sincere, you won't feel authentic showing lots of enthusiasm. Be yourself. Even football coaches differ in their level of arm waving and fiery rhetoric. Some prefer to be steady and consistent in their approach—yet their will to win is rock solid.

So if you are more sincere, you may want to add a bit of drama or interest with the following four techniques.

A client once named these, "Melt in your mouth techniques." Try them on to see which fits. Please consider that anything new will seem awkward at first, so give each a fair chance. Since they're like salt, to spice up your conversation—don't overdo.

Stress—In grade school, we learned that some syllables are stressed. Choose a word to place greater emphasis and let that word stand out in a sentence. The meaning of the sentence changes with the word you choose.

For example:

I love you. (Here I am, the one who loves you!)
I **love** you. (I don't just like you.)
I love **you**. (I don't love someone else.)

Repeat: Take a word or phrase in a sentence that you want others to remember and say it twice. This helps in retention and adds drama. Play with a variety of ways to say this phrase.

Pause: Place a space of silence (2-3 seconds) before or after a word. This space is your pause. It gives the listener time to process, time to question and anticipate what will come next. Pausing demonstrates assurance and control. Enjoy your "words." Honor silence as a blank canvas that displays your message.

Stretch: Find a word that is interesting, important or long and S-T-R-E-T-C-H out the syllables. In the past, we heard this whenever Johnny Carson was introduced and today this technique is used at professional sporting events when the starting line-up is announced.

11) Could you say more about gesturing?

The voice can lie, but the body does not. Gesturing is an indication of what is "going on" with the speaker. When I was in the Toastmasters speech contest a few years ago, I practiced my canned seven-minute speech in front of many audiences. During one such practice, I noticed something odd. This audience didn't smile at me as much as the others. Maybe they were grumpy; maybe they didn't like me or my speech or maybe, because most were engineers, that's the way they process information. Who knows?

My mind was traveling two different directions. Part of me was thinking about what I was saying and the other part was trying to figure out what was wrong. I don't know about you, but I need my whole mind on board when I give a presentation. Had I been video taped that day, you would see a speaker whose movements were stiff and wooden. My anxiety was expressed through my body—my gestures. This is the point: if you want to fix the gestures on the outside, fix the self-consciousness on the inside.

Here are a few suggestions:

1. Watch actors on TV and in the movies. How, when and how much do they gesture? Begin to imitate.
2. Practice with a video camera. Try saying the same sentence using no gestures, an exaggerated gesture and then a normal gesture. A variation: try three completely different gestures with the same sentence.
3. Have a note card or prop in your hand. It will give you an anchor as you begin.

4. Start out your talk with one or two large or powerful "planned" gestures to get you moving and help you release some of your nervous energy.
5. Focus your message on the audience. Forget yourself and give yourself permission to move "naturally."

12) I don't smile much. Is that a problem?

My grandfather used to say, "A little smile goes a long way." If you don't smile very much, you may want to consider this simple, yet powerful skill the next time you speak with someone.

There are smiles that are pasted upon the mouth and smiles that are generated from our true feelings. We may occasionally "Fake it till you make it," however, the goal remains firm: be yourself when you smile.

As I learned in Taekwondo class, when breaking a board, the foot is only the instrument; the whole body needs to be involved in order to be successful. The same is true of a smile—it's hard to be effective in the long run if your heart is not engaged.

What could motivate us to smile more? Here are 30 answers my Personal JAZ^{sm} class gave:

1. To make people feel welcome
2. Shows approval or encouragement
3. Shows enjoyment and excitement
4. Puts people at ease
5. Makes you look younger
6. Gives the impression you are a fun person
7. Is positive reinforcement
8. Indicates that you are a friendly person
9. Sends a signal of warmth and sincerity to others
10. Makes us look relaxed
11. Lets others know we are accessible and approachable

12. Hides nervousness
13. Reactions to you draw *you* out more
14. People will be more willing to listen to you
15. You seem to be interested in your audience
16. You show more energy
17. Gives a feeling of serenity
18. Gives the impression you feel you have many blessings—you're wealthy
19. The audience enjoys seeing a smiling face
20. To have more fun by smiling—makes *me* feel better
21. Personal gauge of what's going on inside—no smile, what's up?
22. Enhances my image
23. It's healthier
24. It's good for business
25. It's the best thing to give away
26. Others treat you better
27. Makes you feel more positive
28. Reminds us to see life as a child
29. Puts people at ease when they first meet us
30. Others more willing to listen to us

13) How can I add more humor to my presentations and my life in general?

The late George Carlin credits his professional success to his *genetic tool box*. He said that he learned to "sing as he talks." Just thinking about him reminds me of the way he viewed everyday life though a curious twist.

Many of us do not tell jokes in social situations. If this describes you, then find a more creative way to add humor. You might not have a genetic tool box, but here are a few tools you can use to lighten up your message:

- Use clever words or words that rhyme.
- Share a poem that fits the topic and assists you in conveying your message.
- Share a story, a note or a letter you received.
- Use a poster or funny slide.
- Use a quote from a famous person—change up the ending.
- Poke fun at yourself or your group.
- Smile and enjoy anything funny the audience may say!

AVOID:
- Putdowns of almost any group—especially if you are NOT a part of that group.
- Anything off-color, tacky, inappropriate or insensitive.
- Anything that makes you feel uncomfortable when you say it.
- When in doubt, don't. If you think you might insult one, you'll probably insult everybody.

The simplest way to bring humor into your life is to laugh. When your inner critic gets too loud—laugh. In fact, laughing clubs began in India and can be found all over the world. People come in, stretch and begin to laugh. In the privacy of your home or car, try it and reap the immediate benefits. Dr. James Peebles, author and lecturer, who lived in the 1800s, said it best, *"Lighten up, for life is a grand adventure!"*

14) How can I begin to develop a style?
Your style becomes a part of you when you repeat elements that work for you. Your style is your signature that comes from trying on who you are. Your style is the result of this formula: Experience + Reflection = Wisdom. Viterbo University professor Carl Koch used to remind us that we

all have experiences, but unless we process what is working and what is not, we become old people with lots of good experiences but no insight into ourselves. Paying attention to ourselves is vital.

When developing a style, choose one or two professionals you admire. Keep a notebook handy to record anything they do or say that appeals to you. Try it on to see if it works for you. If you borrow and adapt from enough people, you'll be on your way to developing your style.

Here are a few ideas to get you started in the category of word choice:

1. When you name items in a list, compose in sets of 3s. Mix up the last word for a twist: blood, sweat and teardrops; faith, hope and determination. The good, the bad and the beautifully challenged.

2. A direct short sentence wakes us up and sticks in our minds. Common examples: "Frankly, my dear, I don't give a damn." "Make my day." "Just do it." When interspersed with longer sentences, these zingers punctuate our communication and bring a delicious variety to what we say. Create your own.

3. Choose two words that play off each other. Our ears love the interplay of opposites: "I'll be here through thick or thin." "In my eyes, she went from being a piece of work to a work of art."

4. Smart words that repeat a sound grab us and feed our imaginations. "He was happy, healthy, and here." "I'm going to investigate, interrogate, like at the Watergate until we see the Pearly Gate!"

CHAPTER 16
FINE TUNING

"Even when we lay down,
we lay down on our own path of life."
— A Native American (Pawnee) Proverb

15) What's the best way to approach the Q & A after my presentation?

Look at the Q & A as the time to really connect with your audience. This is the age of the talk show with participation from both professional and audience members. We, your audience, like to get involved. You, as speaker, will want to be prepared for this part of the presentation even though you can't know exactly which questions may be asked.

The most important concept is—Answer questions in the spirit of understanding. Think in terms of delivering satisfaction to the person with the question, as if you were serving beverages at a party. Make sure they get their favorite kind.

Let's take an example: "How are you doing at work?" You have many choices of how to answer. You could answer with: sarcasm, blunt honesty, humor, sincerity, with great detail or optimism. Which will you choose?

If the group is high in any one of the four modes of communication, you will want to lean that way. If you aren't sure, mix it up a bit.

This is what four modes expect in an answer: Organizers want details, sequence, order, and site references. Be cautious not to spend too much time on any one person in the audience. Instead, give some detail, and then offer to send information to anyone in the group in exchange for their business card.

Action Heroes want the bottom line, without any extra words. You may ask them to clarify so you know the scope of the question. Normally, they already have their own opinion about the topic.

Team Builders will be interested in the human factor and its affect on people, so you might give a short story or example to demonstrate your answer.

Creators have entrepreneurial thoughts. They like possibilities and new information, so be visionary and inspiring.

Organizers and Action Heroes will not use vocal variety, so do not misinterpret what they say as a challenge, that's just the way they communicate. Even if they are challenging you, remain true to yourself with a calm tone. Team Builders and Creators will use more facial and vocal expression. They will expect the same from you.

Here's a check list for you to follow:

- Start with a positive attitude
- Think before you speak
- Avoid "no" and "I don't know " as your first words
- Listen to words/tones/body cues—and clarify
- Be honest and sincere
- Highlight benefits
- Express yourself with power
- Use any "mistake" as a lesson for the next time you speak

16) What is the best way to deal with difficult questions?
As we've said, the questions are exciting and some-times the most challenging part of your presentation, a time

for you to connect with your audience. If you are new to your topic or position, or if the group is one that is a bit out of your comfort zone (or off-the-charts out your comfort zone), your nervousness may get triggered.

The first thing to do is identify what makes a question difficult in the first place. Difficult could be:

- The audience member wants to challenge what you've just said.
- The audience member has a hidden agenda.
- The question reaches beyond your ability and experience.
- The answer is too complex to answer in a short time.
- The answer is embarrassing to you or your company.

When the question is being asked, your job is to listen to the words, tone and body language of the person asking the question. Make sure you hear both what they are saying and not saying; and you understand what is being asked. You may want to request clarification to make sure you understand.

No matter the intention of the question, take the high road. Don't read into the tone of voice; rather, suspect that each question is sincere and use your best judgment. Get in the habit of restating the question you are going to answer. This is desirable for several reasons:

- Without a microphone, not everyone can hear the question.
- It gives you a chance to process your answer.
- If the session is being recorded, those listening to the recording will hear both sides of the conversation.
- You maintain control.

If you have been asked an accusatory question, never repeat the negative words. Also, do not take it personally and respond in a defensive manner. Being defensive will destroy your professionalism, thus canceling the favorable impression you made in your planned remarks. You are in the power position; when attacking one audience member—they all feel wounded.

Unfortunately, this happened during the Q & A portion of a very well-respected professional speaker's presentation. An audience member—let's call her Sally—made an observation about one of the speaker's main points. The speaker could have simply clarified the remark: "Sally, that was not my intent. What I wanted you to hear was…" but instead her defensiveness turned into an all out offensive attack.

It changed the energy in the room and her inner fighter came to the surface, ready to prove she was right and poor Sally was wrong. At one point, a few in the audience cheered at a winning verbal punch from the speaker. I withdrew into my seat—sharing the pain. I wonder how many of the speaker's books Sally bought that day?

A great example of someone who handles the Q & A with ease and grace is Peter Gerdes, CIO of Brain State Technologies®. Peter announced that he would answer questions during his presentation and the group began to participate. Most questions started with "What about..." and "Do you work with..." Some questions sounded confrontational while others were about specific illnesses that I'd not heard about—yet he never missed a beat. He spoke with calm assurance about each body malfunction, with an example, statistics or a story to prove his point. The audience was impressed.

Make your answers conversational yet keep things moving. After all, this is not the time for a one-on-one session or a confrontation. Instead, be firm. Go back to your "themes" or "talking points" (4 or 5 items you believe to be true about your subject). Begin by restating the question, tell your point of view, then explain your reason and give an example that demonstrates your point. Finally, restate your position.

Here's an example:

Question: Why didn't your company endorse the bill that would have saved our neighborhoods?

Answer: The question is about your concern for the safety and well being of our neighborhoods. Our company's mission *is* to be of service to the community. I'm proud to say that last year, we spent $25,000 with 5 cities to plant gardens and we paid for release time for 30 employees to work on the neighborhood playground project. Our company's commitment to this community is demonstrated every day.

Be firm in limiting those who want to dominate the session. Be positive and respectful to everyone. Be the leader by having a prepared ending statement—your parting words.

There are two opportunities for growth here. The first is to anticipate common questions and practice the answers. The second lesson is to remember that we always have a choice to see the questions as threatening and people difficult; or we can treat the whole experience as a game, testing ourselves, thus expanding our thinking—giving us more depth for our next presentation. Even if you disappoint yourself with your answers, the experience is etched in your being and wisdom arms you for the next presentation.

Just as great teachers learn from their students, wise speakers have an opportunity to learn from their audiences. Enter the Q & A portion of your presentation with curiosity and gratitude, and you'll find that your mind is sharper and your answers amaze you!

17) How do you tailor a presentation to fit a diverse audience?

Just as we love the sound of our own names, audiences love tailored presentations. In truth, about 80-85% of what you say will be your tried-and-true presentation. By changing a few visuals and words, you'll gain rapport with the audience. The more rapport, the easier the communication becomes. The categories you choose to tailor may be the same for each presentation and might include any of the following:

- Company name and logo
- Names of people
- Company motto or mission statement
- Something that just happened locally in the company
- Examples of challenging situations in that company
- Their words (do they say client or customer, for example)
- Their heroes (avoid praising their competitors)

If you are likely to have lots of Organizers:
- Give them data to read about their industry
- Print out an agenda with their name and logo
- Be sequential in your talk, refer to one of their processes

If you are likely to have lots of Acton Heroes:
- Let them know up-front how long you will speak
- Emphasize the results they need
- Use shorter, more direct sentences: The bottom line reasons are 1….2….3."

If you are likely to have lots of Team Builders:
- Take the time to say, "Hello, How are you? I've heard _____ about you."

- Use a friendly tone of voice as you tell an industry-related story.
- Emphasize how the data affects people in their company.

If you are likely to have lots of Creators:
- Let them know how the idea is new or unique in their industry.
- Use the word "fun" as it relates to their successes.
- Use color, 3 dimensional or high-tech visuals with names and logos.

If you have a mix of each, and usually you do, provide something for everyone! Be sincere, trust yourself and expand on this list to surprise your audience. A tailored presentation, like a tailored suit—the fit is perfect.

18) What do I need to consider when selecting visuals for my presentation?
Use visuals that you feel comfortable using. What you use depends upon the who, where, and purpose of your speaking engagement. Yet before we move forward, let's get clear about the *why* of visuals themselves. What purpose do they serve?

Presenting a message is a lot like delivering a pizza. The goal is for the great product we took out of *our* oven to arrive at *their* door, hot and in its original form—ready for them to digest. The visual is the object we see, the concrete expression of our words, thoughts and ideas. Just as a picture is worth thousands of words, so is the value of a visual.

This subject is dear to my heart. In third grade, I gave my first speech describing the most exciting adventure of my life. I told about my journey to school one day. On this particular day, I was late getting ready for school, hid behind a tree so the kids who were on the playground (of another school) would not see me, missed the city bus, walked all the way to school—throwing my mom in a panic. The class looked at me with blank stares. My story made no sense to them and *I* assumed that *I was a terrible public speaker.*

The truth is, my audience was made up of children from the small town of Canton, Minnesota, who didn't know about city life in Sioux City, Iowa. They didn't know that there was a public school near my home, yet I attended a private school two miles away. They didn't know that I walked seven blocks and then took the city bus the rest of the way to school.

My audience didn't know what I knew and I didn't know that they didn't know—so I just chatted on about my grand adventure, and they couldn't visualize what I was saying. They looked at me as if I were a crazy person. (Can a whole classroom of 3rd graders be wrong?) If I would have only had one simple map of my route, I could have avoided the confusion as well as the damage done by the self-doubt it caused in my little-girl mind.

Note: In retrospect, I am thankful for that day, because I believe we all have similar stories that are unpleasant, yet they shape our destiny. This is mine.

As an adult, I realize the same is true. During Optio Solutions sales presentations, we can talk for hours about our product, but when the client can see the numbers through showing the charts and graphs, clarity comes to the mind of the business owner. "Ah ha" moments are what we strive to achieve through any visual. We must keep this goal before us as we make choices on the best visuals to use.

Here are six ideas to guide you as you make your own decisions:

1. Make sure the room is dark enough to see the visuals but light enough to write notes and see you, the speaker. This is especially true if you wish to have group participation. If the room cannot be darkened enough to see the visual, use something else rather than spend your time apologizing and frustrating audience members.
2. Keep everything as simple as possible. Make sure that your visual looks clean and uncluttered. Also stick to one or two types of visual. Less is more.
3. Make sure that the words can be read in all parts of the room. The general rule of thumb is no more than six words across and six words down. If you have lots of numbers, use several slides rather than one with 32 columns. Make sure everyone in the room can see.
4. The best visuals are more than words. Use a variety of symbols, charts and pictures. Make them fun. Use color!
5. The speaker will want to connect with the audience not the visual. Look at it occasionally, but remember that it is your tool. In most cases, you will not want to start or end with the visual. The bigger the visual, the smaller the person.
6. Check out your equipment, have spare parts and get set up ahead of time—if possible. Again, the tool should serve you and not the other way around.

Years ago, George Carlin had new material about his dog and cat. His routine lasted for at least ten minutes and was very funny. But after the routine, he showed home slides of what he had just talked about—the audience laughed even louder. The take away is, if my delivery is as polished as a professional comedian, visuals make it just that much better!

19) Is it possible to make highly technical material interesting?

Yes it is. However, never say that your topic is boring or dry. Years ago, when we were building a house, we used to talk with a man who mixed and sold paint. He knew quite a bit about his product and he used to give mini sermons about paint. I didn't understand much of what he said, but I loved to hear him get into the details with such passion.

Be true and passionate about your material. Get into your material while asking yourself why it's important to the audience. The person who asked you to speak (the meeting planner) can also give you insight into the value you'll bring to the audience.

Also, consider the following:

1. Don't read your report. Your technical report will no doubt be very long. In the time allotted you will not be able to read it—nor do you want to insult the group by reading it to them. Instead, highlight the most important points, the most surprising parts, issues surrounding the money—especially if money is to be saved, spent, or an unexpected event is announced. If you were in the audience, what questions would you ask the presenter? The answers to these questions will assist you in knowing what to say. Then choose a systematic way to present.

2. Add examples or stories that are not included in the report. How does it affect people? Animals? The environment? This is a good way to humanize the report.

3. Use flag phrases that say to the audience, "Listen up—here comes the good stuff." If you are speaking to ten people, probably only two or three are listening to you at any one time. As listeners, our minds tend to wander. Bring everyone back with phrases like:

"...and this best part is..."
"My personal favorite is..."
"If you only remember one thing I've said..."
"There are three things that are important here..."
"One interesting thing to note is..."
"If you turn to page 24, second column..."
"And the good news is...."

20) My topic is technical in nature, yet I don't want to talk over my audience. How do I do that?

An important first step in your preparation is to have a thorough discussion regarding the audience with the person who asked you to speak. Find out what they know, what they want to know, what they need to know. The more research you do, the more confident you can be of making the best choices.

Years ago, I was scheduled to speak with a law firm. On my research team were two of the partner's wives and a colleague, a former attorney. They assisted me in the preparation stage. Each gave me helpful advice, including comments about last year's speaker. I merged this information with my material to speak the "language" they would accept and respect.

Another way to keep audiences engaged is to allow their questions during the presentation. Even though they might not be fluent in your topic, they deserve respect. Before you begin, warn them of your passion for the technical aspects of your topic, "So if this happens, please stop me and make me clarify for you."

Use analogies to create pictures in their minds. Analogies are fun and simplify a complicated process for the lay person. You might be thinking, "How can I simplify when the process is so complex?" I agree, yet audiences who are not in your line of work prefer to have a frame of reference. Details become distracting. The analogy gives a way to begin with the known and strategically introduce the unknown. "The TRV units go through a rest period, much like a bear hibernating in winter."

It's alright to use the correct technical word and then explain it. "The vat was filled with AZDTRE, which, as many of you know, is a soft metal mixture." Notice how the clause, *as many of you know*, shows respect to those in the audience who might know the terms.

Some speakers wish to give definitions for the three or four terms they use. This can be done verbally, in the beginning of the talk or on a handout—again, near the beginning is best to establish a joint language.

The key is to respect the audience, then focus on listening, and respond in a way that will assist you in accomplishing your presentation goals.

Part 5
AM I ROCK
SOLID CONFIDENT?

"All the great ones look at the challenges
in their lives as a way to test their characters."

CHUCK LONG, FORMER QUARTERBACK FOR
UNIVERSITY OF IOWA, PROFESSIONAL ATHLETE
AND COLLEGIATE COACH.

CHAPTER 17
A LIFE OF CONFIDENCE

*"We will be known forever by
the tracks we leave."*
— A Native American (Dakota) Proverb

With each new day, we get another chance to be confident. The goal is to have assurance and poise without arrogance. Rik, a business associate, once said, "To me, passion for something and pride, although dangerous in some respects, are required when you do what you love." Some of us arrogantly slip into the trap of taking ourselves too seriously. The writer of the following statement speaks of the danger in pride.

"... Anyone who specializes in anything has to be ignorant of many other things in order to win status as an expert, real or self-anointed. But a professional gets so accustomed to being taken seriously when he's asked for advice within the realm of his specialty, that eventually he comes to assume that people will be interested in and benefit from everything he says about anything."

Oprah Winfrey, whose popularity and power seem unlimited, remains grounded and real. In a recent television interview, she rejected the suggestion to run for president. She said that politics was not for her; she knew how to *stay in her lane*. Her example reminds us to retain confidence, yet be faithful to our purpose and mission.

A healthy child is generally more ready to learn than the average adult. When instructing students in Taekwondo class, one difference was revealed clearly.

When demonstrating a hand movement to children, we'd say, "Do this," and the children did what they were shown. Simple, clean and ready for the next step.

When demonstrating the same hand movement to typical adults, their response to, "Do this," was hesitation. Their minds process the implications, "Now, what does this do for me? Why am I doing it? Is this the right technique? It seems hard. Does he know who I am? Will it make me look foolish? By the way, *what did you tell me to do?*"

This myriad of doubt takes energy and time, making it impossible to focus on the original instructions. We know we're making progress when we are passionately involved in each moment. Before entering a practice hall in Taekwondo, the students remove their shoes. In a similar spirit, we know we are on the right track when we are able to confidently check suspicions and doubts—our egos—at the door when being instructed. Instead of "Yes, but…" we are able to open our hearts to learning and say, "Thank you."

I was a first-degree black belt the night I was asked to break my first brick, which stirred memories of breaking my first board three years before. Back then, I didn't know if I'd be able to keep up with the others—and to be truthful, I was never an extraordinary student. But I loved it anyway. At first it gave me the chance to participate in my sons' lives and eventually I was there for myself, to achieve a goal and a new way of trusting myself.

Master Bruce got the wild idea to have his black belt adults break bricks with their hands. I heard the rumor, so the night the bricks were brought into the room, I knew what was coming. I did not have the Chuck Long attitude of welcoming the challenge, yet for three years, I had taken baby steps in trusting myself—it was my final test.

By this time, the class grew to 50 students. They formed a large circle around the edge of the gym and the bricks were placed on top of two columns of patio blocks. Again, I was called first. Master Bruce showed me how to stand and where to strike. This time, there would be no second chances. I'd either break the brick or I'd break my hand. I'll never forget his words, "You've done many difficult things since you were a white belt. I am very proud of you and I know you can do this, too."

Sometimes we need to have someone believe in us before we believe in ourselves. Sometimes we do what stretches our level of comfort. Always we need to let the trust of others sink in, allowing it to become our own.

On that occasion, I did just that. I stood the way I was told to stand. I measured the distance with a few practice swings and most importantly, I pulled up *every bit* of strength my body could muster. The energy came bursting out from the core of my being in the loudest, longest, most determined "I-AAAAH" of my life. My hand was merely the instrument that sent the brick to the floor; I stood there looking at it in disbelief (Was I waiting for the instant replay?). They finally persuaded me go back to the circle so the next student could take a turn.

What can be learned from this experience? What "bricks" have you faced?

It's all about connecting the dots; connecting our experiences with our lessons. It's noticing that the same stumbling blocks come to us through different people, under a different disguise. Realizing that our knowledge accumulates, we are able to bring so much more to the table each time we approach a new situation. It might be a presentation, taking on a new career, or taking a risk to achieve a goal. Silently confidence grows.

How do you know if you are confident? How do you know when you have arrived? Do we ever get to a point of being carefree, like a child?

We are humans working out this confidence puzzle. The late John O'Donohue tells us that humans are clay beings and it's silly to think of us as perfect creatures. As we grow in confidence, the scales begin to tip. Imperfections challenge us more than they bother us. As challenges arrive at the doorstep, we don't go to pieces or fall into our familiar patterns of fear. Like a thermostat, we program our minds to keep confidence levels stable. No more drama, mood swings and panic attacks.

We know we're doing well when we feel anticipation for each day because we believe that whatever curve ball is thrown our way, we'll be able to handle it. When we feel insecure, we calmly notice the feeling and use the tools we have learned to keep us on a steady path of growth.

True freedom comes when we can interact with the beautiful, the rich, the brainy and the powerful—with ease and grace. A new world opens up when we are quick to forgive ourselves for mistakes and learn to laugh at the way we take ourselves too seriously. Once we walk through that door and taste the sweetness of peace in our being, we'll never want to live another way.

Confidence is confirmed when we realize we are not afraid to know the truth and are better able to tactfully communicate with others—to get to the bottom of a situation. Extra pressure is removed when we stop measuring our self-worth by the responses of the people around us and events of the day. It feels like the vine that used to be wrapped around us, constricting our movement, has been magically cut away, freeing us.

Maybe the best part is the awareness of joy in our lives. We don't have to be doing anything special to be happy. We don't have to be with anyone to feel we belong. Instead of feeling "by ourselves," we feel "with ourselves" everywhere we go, 24/7.

The urge to meddle in the lives of others or fix everyone around us disappears. Because we have our own goals to accomplish, we *mind our own business* and if asked, give advice from a grounded impartial perspective. When we see a frog with a pretty hat, we rejoice with that frog and feel truly blessed to be able to witness such beauty.

This is freedom. This is the sweet taste of ourselves as pure as the day we were born. We become as poised as the mountain that remains solid through blizzards, forest fires and tornadoes. We are powerful beyond our comprehension.

With this confidence we are able to do the work we came to do. No one can predict the days ahead, and yet with rock solid confidence, our assurance is in the knowledge that no one on the planet is like us. No one has our eyes, our experiences, our gifts to create the life we choose. Choose well and often.

People and Books

The following is a list of people and books I recommend for your future growth and development. Some are directly related to making presentations while others will inspire your personal development. All authors are authentic and cherished.

Ailes, Roger. *You are the Message: Getting What You Want by Being Who You Are.*

Benton, D.A. *Lions Don't Need to Roar: Using the Leadership Power of Professional Presence to Stand Out, Fit In and Move Ahead.*

Berg, Karen and Andrew Gilman. *Get to the Point: How to Say what You Mean and Get What You Want.*

Brenner, Dr. Helene G. *I Know I'm in There Somewhere: A Woman's Guide to Finding Her Inner Voice and Living A Life of Authenticity.*

Coelho, Paul. *The Alchemist.*

Connor, Steven Eric. *Eyes of Love: Envision the Spirit of Your Soul* and *Fearless and Free in Love, the Enneagram.*

Frankl, Viktor E. *Man's Search for Meaning.*

Ford, Debbie. *The Right Questions, Ten Essential Questions to Guide You to an Extraordinary Life.*

Frick, Don M. *Robert K. Greenleaf: A Life of Servant Leadership.*

Gerdes, Lee. *Limitless You: the Infinite Possibilities of a Balanced Brain.*

Hammerschlag, Dr. Carl A. *The Dancing Healers: A Doctor's Journey of Healing with Native Americans.*

Hillman, Ralph. *Delivering Dynamic Presentations: Using Your Voice and Body for Impact.*

Loomis, Logan. *Both Sides Win!* and *Getting the People Equation Right: How to get the Right People in the Right Jobs and Keep Them.*

Lowe, Robert. *Improvisation, Inc.: Harnessing Spontaneity to Engage People and Groups.*

Luntz, Dr. Frank. *Words That Work: It's Not What You Say, It's What People Hear.*

Markova, Dawna. *I will not Die an Unlived Life: Reclaiming Purpose and Passion.*

O'Donohue, John. *Anam Cara: A book of Celtic Wisdom.*

Radmacher, Mary Anne. *Courage Doesn't Always Roar* and *Lean forward into your Life: begin each day as if it were on purpose.* Conari Press. Note: All books Mary Anne writes are spectacular.

Rosenberg, Arlene. *Say It, See It, Be It: How Visions & Affirmations Will Change Your Life.*

Ruiz, Don Miguel. *The Four Agreements* and *The Fifth Agreement.*

Severson, Rob. *Connecting Peace, Purpose & Prosperity: A Survival Guide and Memoir.*

Williams, Rev. Cynthia. *The Eye of the Dolphin* and *Jesus, My Beloved Connection to Humanity and the Sea.*

Wydro, Kenneth. *Think On Your Feet.*

Zona, Guy A. *The Soul Would Have No Rainbow If the Eyes Had No Tears: And Other Native American Proverbs.*

WITH GRATITUDE AND LOVE

No book is created in isolation. In naming some, I leave out most. This book has been evolving my whole life, encompassing my lessons—the ones I've taught and the ones brought to me through my challenges and insecurities. Through questions and questioning my purpose, the core of this book was born. So my first gratitude is to my Creator who let this adventure unfold.

I'm in awe of the number of students and teachers I've had in my lifetime—most especially my children Mike (Tinisha, Cam and Tru) and Scott Roelofs and their father, Jon. My sibs—Doc Len, Ralph, John, Mary, Karen, Ruth and Laura—were the perfect companions to begin my journey and engaged Joyce, Ellen, Dave and Dan plus amazing nieces and nephews.

I'm daily grateful to my dog Jazz, a Yorkie who is never afraid to play with the big dogs. While he's not much of a reader, I want to give him public credit for the way he demonstrates the spirit of total confidence I aspire to create in my life.

My other families from Harmony High School, Winona State University, Viterbo University at Prairiewoods, provided formal education; as well as Master David Bruce and his Taekwondo family.

Blessings to my K.J. sisters of P.E.O. for financially supporting my dream of higher education.

Dr. Ralph Hillman, Robert Lindsey-Nassif, Samantha Needham, Logan Loomis, Halsey Munson, Lisa Edwards, Don Frick, Deb Frese, Joanne Hagedorn, Steven Eric Connor,

Mary Anne Radmacher, Robert Lowe and Terry Buske, for coaching me through the various stages of professionalism.

Toastmasters International Sunrise Marion group for helping me stand a little taller and providing me hours of pure joy on Wednesday morning. National Speakers Association for invaluable opportunities to view the world from the top shelf.

My clients who honored me by opening their lives and their hearts in my office; your courage and willingness to bring value to the world are my greatest rewards.

My faithful book creation team with graphic angel Crystal McMahon, and Don Enevoldsen with his huge heart and technical expertise.

And finally, to Rev. Cynthia Williams (and Yoda), for answering my call and for repeating the words, "How's your book coming?"

I love you dearly.

ABOUT THE AUTHOR

Jan Whalen, MASL is the founder and President of Personal JAZ^{sm}, a training and seminar company. With a background in sales, public relations, education and community service, her mission is to live with passion. She has a unique talent for finding gold in her clients, associates, and friends.

A native Midwesterner, she followed her children to Arizona where she is called Granjama by two extraordinary grandchildren. Before leaving Iowa, she received a Master of Arts Degree in Servant Leadership from Viterbo University and a black belt in Taekwondo under the leadership of Master David Bruce.

Rock Solid Confidence

FOR MORE INFORMATION

Contact Jan about quantity discounts
for this book as well as
private presentation coaching,
keynotes, seminars and workshops.

Contact her by email:

jan@personaljaz.com

or by phone: 623 466-5067

CPSIA information can be obtained at www.ICGtesting.com
Printed in the USA
LVOW080210280512

283520LV00001B/2/P